Richard Wagner
Rudolf Steiner
&
Allegories of The Ring

From the Mundane to the Esoteric

George Hastings

B&H Bennett &
Hastings Publishing

For the four *Ring Cycle* operas, page number references are
to Andrew Porter's 1977 translation published by W.W. Norton,
assigned ISBN 0-393-00867-3.

For *Parsifal*, page number references are to Andrew Porter's
translation as it appears in the 1995 *German Opera Libretti*, (a volume in the series *The German Library*), edited by James Steakley,
assigned ISBN 0-8264-0739-0 (paperback) and ISBN 0-8264-
0738-2 (hardcover).

ISBN 978-1-934733-69-1

Richard Wagner
Rudolf Steiner
&
Allegories of The Ring

From the Mundane to the Esoteric

An extensive cast of characters is included at the back of this book.

"I want to speak to you today about the truths of occultism and of theosophy, relating what I have to say with Richard Wagner's *Parsifal*. For there is a deep connection between the artistic work of Wagner and the spiritual movement of the present day that is known as Theosophy. That there is in Wagner and in his works a very large measure of occult power, is something that mankind is gradually learning to realize. And in the future something further will also become clear to us; namely, that there lived in Wagner a great deal more than he himself could have knowledge of. This is, in truth, the secret of many a work of art, that a force and a power live in it of which its creator knows nothing."

Rudolf Steiner
29 July 1906

Contents

FOREWORD

A few years ago I made a decision to make a major life change. In order to do this I had to give up my extensive library of books pertaining to, among other subjects, art, history, philosophy, religion, current events, and many of the lectures and written works of Rudolf Steiner. Although I do not regret my decision it has made life a little more difficult at times. The biggest drawback is that I cannot make detailed references and citations which the public, and especially academia, wants and expects. In this book I list only my main sources in the text, to assist any reader who wants more information.

I have used many authors whose research I value but whose conclusions I disagree with. One example is Jared Diamond, who wrote the Pulitzer Prize winning book *Guns, Germs and Steel.* He brilliantly explained how human thinking took place along what I would call *mechanical* paths. He never speaks of spiritual influences. In this I feel he is missing the bigger picture and I add *spiritual* evolutionary aspects to his findings. It would be a mistake to think that because I use the benefits of his research I agree totally with his conclusions.

This brings us to Wagner. One of the big problems I have when lecturing on Wagner or even discussing him openly is the reaction of people who refuse to consider anything he said or produced because he was an anti-Semite. My response to this is, first, that we have a lot to learn from those with whom we disagree: excluding them from our consciousness does not seem wise. Second, it is a well-established fact that Wagner had many Jewish friends and helpers, and it seems unlikely that this would have been the case if he was the anti-Semitic monster many people make him out to be. Wagner did not hate anyone for being Jewish. What he did despise was dogmatism in any form. As a result, Wagner disliked many religions, but he did feel that Judaism was an especially dogmatic and authoritarian religion. As a result, he believed that it went against the cause of freedom. Late in his life, Wagner endorsed Christianity; but even then, his Christianity was not the traditional, exoteric Christianity. It was an esoteric Christianity in which each individual had to find the answers within themselves, without dogma.

I would like the reader to bear in mind that references and citations prove nothing. For every reference or citation I could give, if I still had my library, I, and others, could give a contrary one. The reader must take responsibility for judging my work and the works of others, even if it means labeling what an author says as true, false, or possible. We do not live in a black and white world, despite the fact that many cultural leaders try to make it appear that we do. There is nothing the matter with concluding that an opinion or theory is a "maybe": maybe it is right, maybe it isn't. To eliminate the "maybes" would be to structure authoritarian dogma. Human thinking has, I hope, grown beyond that.

The trend in human thinking is to balance intellect and intuition, art and science, right brain and left brain. We have lived in an intellectualized, left brain culture too long. It is time to develop further. Those who do not realize this will be, pardon the pun, left behind.

I would also like to point out that, with esoteric literature every answer brings up more questions. This drives some people nuts and brings great joy to others. To be happy as a student of esoteric literature, accept that mastery of your topic will always be a few steps ahead of you. Seeking and finding is an ongoing process. I certainly do not claim to be conveying complete information on the subjects in this book. I hope, though, that some readers will go on to delve further, if they haven't already.

INTRODUCTION

Life is a two-edged sword. That old saying has become cliché, but it's true. What cannot be used for either good or evil? Even love: even it can be manipulated, and often is, to serve forces which do not support a person's higher nature. Just think of all the wars that have been passionately fought by two forces claiming their motives are the love of God. A ring can also have two edges. Wedding rings are symbols of the uniting of two people. The concept of uniting that which is within a ring can be considered one of the edges of a ring. On the other edge, a ring separates. Surrounding something with a ring, such as a castle with a moat, separates that which is within *the ring* from that which is without. Wagner's *Ring Cycle* operas are about taking what was once an all-encompassing spiritual ring and transforming it into a condensed physical ring of isolation. The all-encompassing ring represents universal wisdom. *The ring* of isolation represents the force of extreme individualism, the selfish ego. This ego is caught up in itself. It cares naught for anyone else.

Wagner chooses, as his tale's main symbol, a ring of gold. In his day, the chemical element gold had very little practical value beyond minor industrial use and for dentistry; but gold was representative of money and, therefore, sometimes hoarded. For some, à la King Midas, the ultimate goal would be to hoard all the gold in existence, despite the reasonable assumption that this would do nobody, especially the hoarder, any good. A hoarder of gold would be psychologically and spiritually separated from the rest of humanity; and very likely characterized as hedonistic, materialistic, power hungry, money hungry, and destructive toward everything outside of his own "ring." What, then, would motivate or compel someone to hoard gold? Some might believe that such a ring would bring security, but that would be a misconception. What it would bring is power: the power to control the world on the physical plane, even if this proves ultimately self-destructive.

Wagner's *Ring* is allegorical; its meaning goes deeper than the storyline, but like a good fairy-tale its storyline weaves a memorable tale. *The Ring cycle* can be enjoyed as a good yarn, interpreted as an exposé on the ills of capitalism, or, viewed on an even higher level as a treasury of secret spiritual beliefs concerning the evolution of humanity. Many years ago, before the days of Dan Brown's *The Da Vinci Code* and so many other "pop" stories about secret societies, I recognized that there were many allegorical (secret) messages in Wagner's operas pertaining to evolution and the spiritual world. Since then I have continually looked for, and found, many more of them. As this was going on I also became aware that many other artists in various milieus did the same thing. Over the years I focused on some of the works of Homer, Michelangelo, and Mozart along with Wagner. What surprised me most was that all of the artists were telling a version of the same story. They told their story in pictorial format, a way that appeals to what we now refer to as the right side of the brain. My research left no doubt in my mind that these similar messages were the same as the teachings of the early twentieth century physicist and philosopher Rudolf Steiner.

Unlike the artists I studied, most of Rudolf Steiner's presentations were in the form of the spoken or written word. By using an intellectual approach Steiner explained details about the spiritual world that pictorial and artistic methods have trouble conveying. Steiner, however, taught from the perspective of *both* the right and left sides of the brain; that is, he directed his teachings to both picture consciousness and intellectual consciousness. The way he did that was to give details but spread those details out in several ways within a bigger picture, essentially forcing the learner to gather information from among various resources and develop their own conclusions. This method goes against the currently popular deductive learning techniques, which are primarily interested in conveying facts that can be stored in a computer. Steiner taught about nearly all aspects of culture. In spite of the fact that he wrote over thirty books and gave over 6,000 lectures he never claimed to be providing all-encompassing or complete information. He wanted others to carry on his work. This book is an attempt to add further information to his teachings by describing many of the hidden spiritual insights presented in *The Ring*

CHAPTER 1
SATAN AND LUCIFER

The Ring is about what the Bible calls the "fall from Paradise." The fall can be thought of in terms of the "forest and the trees," with the forest representing the spiritual world, and the trees representing the physical world. It was mankind's transition from the unity and oneness of the spiritual world to the separation and isolation of the individualized parts and pieces of the physical, earthly world. Bear in mind that the earthly realm which we live in is actually *spirit*, but the fall represents a shift in our consciousness, or our ability to perceive the earthly realm with our spirit consciousness. The fact that we do not see it that way is because our consciousness plays tricks on us. Spiritual consciousness and earthly consciousness are two types of consciousness.

The Rhinegold is the first of four *Ring Cycle* operas. It begins with the Rhinemaidens frolicking in the waters of the River Rhine. Beginning in water is an allegorical way of expressing the state of consciousness that existed before the present. According to Steiner the solar system as we know it did not start with a "big bang." It started out in a state that can best be described as "warmth," then condensed into a state best described as "gaseous," then condensed further into a state we can call "fluid," and gradually condensed into the physical state we can call "solid." These states – "warmth," "gaseous," "fluid," "solid" – are really describing states of consciousness. Metaphorically speaking, fire represents warmth, air represents the state of consciousness esotericists describe as gaseous; water represents the consciousness state described as fluid; and earth represents what esotericists call the solid state. *The Rhinegold* starts out at the end of the period of the fluid state, a period esoterically associated with legends of Atlantis. All ancient cultures have stories about the water and floods.

Steiner wrote some commentary on Wagner's *Ring*, most of which appeared in periodicals. According to Steiner the Rhinemaidens are pre-human beings. In the libretto of *The Rhinegold* they had the task of guarding the *sleeping gold*, which, according to Steiner, was universal wisdom as it existed *before* what is called the "fall" in the Bible. Along comes Alberich, a creepy dwarf who wants to play with the Rhinemaidens. He even hopes to find love with them, but his idea of love is strictly lust on the physical level. They not only reject him, they thoroughly humiliate him. As the opera stage becomes increasingly bright Alberich asks the Rhinemaidens what is happening. They explain that sunlight is "greeting the gold" and *the sleeper* is being called to awaken. Esoterically this means humanity is about to evolve (awaken) into a new and higher state of consciousness in which clarity and understanding are important aspects. The Rhinemaidens tell Alberich that the golden radiance sleeps and wakes in turn. Alberich is not impressed and says it is worthless. By that point in the opera the light has gotten brighter, and it actually condenses on the top of a rock in the form of a huge gold nugget. The Rhinemaidens tell Alberich that whoever captures the gold, makes it into a ring, and renounces love will rule the earth. This perks his interest. If he cannot find love with the Rhinemaidens he will settle for the gold and its power. He will even be able to buy love, he thinks. With an incredible display of will he scurries up the slippery rock, steals the gold and rejects love. Alberich is a metaphor for the evil spirit which controls humanity's materialistic and monetary nature. He is the first of the three powerful spirits whom Wagner portrays as vying for control of the world. Steiner calls him Ahriman, and Ahriman is another name for Satan.

The second spirit in this trio who seek the gold is Loge. According to the libretto he is a liar, a trickster, affiliated with fire (which will become very significant as the story progresses). Wagner also tells us that Loge's advice becomes more valuable when it is patiently sought, and that Loge recognizes the importance of love (28-29). Loge wants to steal the gold back from Alberich so it can be returned to the Rhinemaidens, who would then keep it in their waters forever (32). He recognizes the gold was nothing more than a toy for the Rhinemaidens (30) but he also knows it brings eternal youth to those who have it (33). Note that Loge wants to preserve consciousness in the state in which it was before Alberich stole it. In other words Loge seeks a return to the state which existed before the "fall." This point cannot be overemphasized. Steiner calls this spirit Lucifer.

The relationship between Loge and Alberich becomes apparent when they confront each other, and Loge says:

Why do you bark?
In chilly caves
you shivered and froze:
Who gave you light
and who lit your fires then?
Was Loge not once your friend?
What use are your forges
till they are heated by me?
I am your kinsman
and once was kind:
For that you owe me your thanks! (44-45)

Steiner was the first to outwardly point out that Lucifer, the devil, is a spirit distinct from Satan. Traditionally humanity believed itself plagued by one evil spirit given many names, such as Lucifer, the devil, or Satan. In the past, when life was simpler, further distinction was hardly relevant. Today that has changed. The power of the spirit of materialism, Satan, is so pronounced that it needs to be distinguished from that of Lucifer. They are opposites. Wagner has already alluded to the fact that Alberich (Satan) is loveless. From Loge we learn that Alberich dwells in a cave, is very cold, and does not have a light of his own. In the Bible Lucifer is referred to as the light bearer. He too does not have a light of his own but carries another's light. Lucifer is closely associated with the "Light" while Satan is the Spirit of Darkness. Lucifer is affiliated with the non-physical spiritual world, and Ahriman is attached to the physical realm. Steiner's descriptions of Ahriman and Lucifer and Wagner's portrayals of Alberich and Loge are completely in accord.

Lucifer is artistic and intuitive. Ahriman is intellectual and calculating. Their characteristics are numerous, but to use modern psychological terminology Lucifer has qualities strongly related to our right brain faculties and Ahriman with the left brain's faculties. This may be a generalization but it carries a lot of weight and may be a useful way to differentiate them in the present age. Today most teaching is done using left brain methods (Ahrimanic), although a trend away from that has started in some milieus. Wagner taught through right brain picture consciousness (Luciferic) with mythology and allegories. Steiner balanced the two sides. In his book *A Philosophy of Freedom*, also sometimes called *The Philosophy of Spiritual Activity*, he carefully explains the need to use both sides of the brain in order to arrive at truth. He does not use the terms right and left sides of the brain, he uses the words "concepts" and "percepts." (When asked what he believed would be his most important contribution to humanity Steiner replied it would be that book.)

The beginning of *The Rhinegold* sets the stage for a battle over the use of divine wisdom. The first combatants, Alberich and Loge, are analogous to Ahriman/Satan (Alberich) and Lucifer (Loge). Will divine wisdom be held hostage by Alberich, who has foresworn love and hoards it solely for power? Or will it be

returned to the Rhinemaidens, as Loge wishes, grant-
ing them eternal beauty and youth; essentially revers-
ing the hands of time? And is such a return to Paradise
even possible, or is a more complex redemption process
demanded?

Enter the gods. The course of divine wisdom will
wend its way through the final days of a race of gods
led by a mighty but flawed warrior-king, Wotan, whose
clairvoyance (i.e. spiritual vision) is represented by his
having lost one of his two eyes. Wotan is the first opera character with whom most humans quite readily
identify. I will explore his make-up and story in depth
over the next few chapters, but for the purposes of this
chapter, suffice it to say that he relies on Loge for certain accomplishments and strategies.

At the end of *The Rhinegold* Wotan leads the other
gods across a rainbow bridge to Valhalla, where they
will be "safe from fear and dread." The rainbow aspect
indicates they are going to another realm, a spiritual
world, where all but one of the gods seems to think
they will be free from the problems of the physical
realm; as if they could sweep the problem of the gold,
which now carries a curse with it, under the rug. The
only one who faces up to the fact that something is still
wrong is Loge (Lucifer).

Loge knows the gods are wrong about the nature of
Valhalla, but he is undecided as to what to do about it.
Because he has helped them get the gold back the other
gods think Loge has been tamed, but they are wrong.

Loge, aware of the gods' mistaken beliefs about life in the spiritual realm, may do a number of things. He makes the audience aware of this by observing that he has *not been tamed* as the gods believe. This characterization is very similar to Rudolf Steiner's descriptions of Lucifer. According to Steiner, Lucifer will act any way he wants unless he has been redeemed, a subject which will be discussed in depth later in this book. Even then, he will act in destructive ways in regards to people who have not "redeemed" him. At the end of *The Rhinegold*, Loge crosses the rainbow bridge with the gods, but he makes no promises as to what he will do next.

Sidebar: According to Rudolf Steiner there are three levels of evil spirits with which we have to contend. They are essentially fallen angels, fallen archangels and fallen archai. The fallen archai, Steiner calls azures. They are out to destroy the will and work primarily though drugs.

Chapter 2
Wotan and Lucifer

To paraphrase Steiner, Lucifer is an evil spirit who works against us when his influence is unchecked, but when we take control of him he assists us in our quest for higher consciousness and he becomes a good spirit. Humanity's task includes the development of the ability to harness Lucifer's powers on a higher, spiritual and moral level. On a lower level Lucifer tempts us to give in to selfish and sensual desires in an unrestrained, harmful manner. Mastering Lucifer means controlling, not squelching, our emotional drives and using them in a positive manner. As we learn to master these desires we master Lucifer and actually redeem him. He then helps us to reach higher levels of consciousness, which includes that level that provides proper entrance to the spiritual world.

One of the prime weaknesses Lucifer preys upon is pride. In the evolving relationship between the god Wotan and Loge, Wagner has created a great metaphor for the struggle to control Lucifer. The relationship between Wotan and Loge is in complete accord with the teachings of Rudolf Steiner regarding the relationship of humanity to Lucifer.

Wotan is the third of the three spirits who will vie for the gold in *The Rhinegold*. Wagner portrays him as the leading "old" god; that is, the leader of gods in an era that is passing. It does not take long to learn that Wotan, although a god, is fallible. He has commissioned two Giants to build a home for the gods; a castle, which he calls Valhalla. It is a place where Wotan's human soldiers who have fallen in combat can be placed as a reward for their superior service. We meet Wotan in Scene **, when the castle has just been completed. Wotan is very proud of it; so proud that he fails to remember the price he has promised to pay for it. He has, in fact, promised the Giants his sister-in-law, Freia, the goddess of youth and beauty, as payment.

Wotan's wife, Fricka, is rightfully upset about her husband's promise to the Giants, and she lets him know it! Wotan tells Fricka not to worry because Loge is coming (21). Fricka shows her disdain for Loge by calling him an infamous rogue. It was Loge who talked Wotan into making the contract with the Giants with Freia as payment (106), and Fricka reminds Wotan that Loge has harmed the gods many times. She cannot understand why he, Wotan, continues to depend upon Loge.

Wotan has indeed had a difficult time learning how to deal with Loge (Lucifer) (250).Wotan, however, justifies his actions by explaining that when the simple truth is adequate he can handle the situation on his own, but that when guile and deceit are needed, as they are in order to transform the hatred of his enemies, Loge is required (22). Two interesting points are made here. First, Loge's tactics include the use of "guile and deceit" (22). Second, Wotan recognizes the need to re-direct or transform the negative energy of his foes (22).

The second point is a basic teaching of Steiner. We do not want to kill our enemies: we want to help them transform themselves, without infringing on their freedom, so that their energy, a two-edged sword, is used for good[1]. Steiner also teaches that the "good" gods cannot use evil methods. What they can do is channel their efforts so that some good can result from evil. For example, if an army is going to attack its enemies there might be several points at which the attack could take place. The "good" spirits may not be able to prevent the attack, but they may be able to direct it to a location or time where less harm, or, hopefully, good will result.

Unfortunately, when Wotan takes Loge's advice on how to rescue his sister-in-law, Freia, from the agreement he has made with the Giants he uses negative means. The consequences are grave.

In Scene 2 of *The Rhinegold*, the Giants who have built Valhalla come for their payment. Wotan tries to double-talk them out of the agreement but they, as primitive as they may be, do not buy his suggestions (23). The Giants tell Wotan that they bargained freely and have kept their part of the agreement. If Wotan does not keep his word, war will result. The two sides are at a stalemate, and Wotan realizes that he cannot

---

[1] The Manichean principles, which will be discussed again, are based on this principle.

save Freia by using truthful means. Loge is needed again!

Wotan confronts Loge, blaming him for the mess, and Loge tries to double-talk his way out of responsibility for the situation. The gods call him a liar (28). Wotan already knows Loge's skills at guile and deceit, and he consults Loge again. Loge suggests that the two of them steal the gold back from Alberich (32). Without much appearance of a moral struggle, Wotan agrees. There is no hint of redemption in this arrangement. Wotan has decided to put Loge's suggestions to work for a lower purpose, hopeful of a simple antidote to his troubles.

Together, Wotan and Loge descend into Nibelheim, the underworld and the domain of Alberich. They intend to steal the gold and turn it over to the Giants in exchange for Freia. The music that accompanies their descent to Nibelheim is memorable and remarkable for its being characterized by the striking of anvils[2]. After having stolen the gold Alberich has used its power to enslave his fellow Niblungs. He mercilessly forces them to mine gold for him, which he then has the craftier among them forge into powerful objects. Alberich now possesses a gold ring that makes the wearer invincible and a tarnhelm (or helmet) that can make him invisible or transmogrify its wearer into whatever form they desire.

---

[2] Wagner was inspired by the sounds of a blacksmith's shop in his neighbored.

The way Loge manipulates Alberich reveals a lot about his character. After Wotan and Loge descend to Nibelheim they confront Alberich. Wotan asks:

> But what's the use of your wealth?
> In joyless Nibelheim,
> With gold there's nothing to buy! (46)
> Alberich responds:
> Gold can be mined here,
> and gold can be stored here,
> deep in Nibelheim's caves.
> Then with my wealth
> from the darkness I'll rise,
> rise and be master of all things:
> the whole wide world
> I'll buy for myself with the treasure! (47)

Perhaps this is Wagner's comment on the gold standard, which ruled the central banks (e.g. the European, U.K. and American economies) of his day. Certainly, his depiction of gold hoarded underground is reminiscent of bank vaults and national treasuries where gold is stored underground and never sees the light of day. And Alberich's character brings to mind people who have exhibited insatiable greed; rulers and business people, as well as common people, whose souls have been traded away in a fruitless pursuit for gold. Alberich is proud of his hoarded wealth, so proud that he is obsessed.

Alberich tells Wotan and Loge:

Once I renounced all joys of love.
All those who live,
all shall renounce them!
Enchanted by gold,
your greed for gold shall enslave you ...
Beware! Beware!
For first your men
shall yield to my might,
then your lovely women,
who despise me and jeer,
shall grant to Alberich's force
what love could not win!
Ha ha ha!
You have been warned!
Beware!
Beware of my armies of night!
Beware the day when the Niblung's gold
shall vanquish the world! (47)

At this Wotan gets a little testy. But Loge interjects

"Try to be patient!" (48)

We have already heard Wotan say:

(Loge's) advice
is worth all the more,
when we wait on his words (28)

Wagner repeats the lesson that in order to use Lucifer (Loge) in a constructive way we must be patient. The stage is now set for Loge to take charge.

Loge steps between Alberich and Wotan and goes into a lengthy dissertation about how fantastically great Alberich is, but Loge ends it with a warning that a thief might steal *the ring* from Alberich while the mighty Niblung sleeps. Alberich discounts the warning and reiterates how powerful he is: he can even change shape and become invisible. Loge again praises him saying, among other things, that Alberich's power could make him "everlasting" (49). Alberich doesn't swallow the bait, but he retorts that he doesn't boast like Loge. Loge then dares Alberich to prove that he has the powers he has described. Alberich accuses Loge of being full of pride, and then tells him to name the shape he wants him to take. The bickering continues as Loge passes the buck back to Alberich telling *him* to choose, that Loge just wants to be awestruck by the change. So Alberich turns into an enormous, ferocious dragon. Loge feigns terror. Wotan laughs.

Alberich, returned to his normal form, says, "Now do you believe me?" (50). Loge butters him up some more and insinuates that he doesn't think Alberich could do the opposite and become a tiny creature. The proud Alberich then turns himself into a tiny toad. At Loge's suggestion Wotan quickly puts his foot on the now tiny Alberich, and Loge captures him. Loge and Wotan then steal the gold.

First Luciferic pride got the best of Wotan, now it has caused Alberich's downfall. In our world that happens all the time. How many wars have been lost because a power hungry ruler spread his army out too thin? How many thieves have gotten caught because they could not stop stealing, even though they had more money than they could spend?

Wotan and Loge carry the gold back to the domain of the gods and negotiate the return of Freia, but not without a murder occurring in the process[3]. Wotan and the gods then ascend to Valhalla, all of them ignorant of the consequences that will follow them there. As mentioned earlier, even Wotan remains ignorant of Loge's state of mind as *The Rhinegold* ends.

In the second opera, *The Valkyrie*, more subtle clues are given about Wotan and his relationship to Loge. Wotan has had to admit that, whatever he does, he cannot correct the mistakes he has made. The only way out is to "make" a free person, one who has no attachments to the gods. Wotan sets out on a totally unselfish quest to make that happen.

Wotan altruistically wants his earthly son, Siegmund, to do what he has been unable to do. Wotan thrusts a sword which contains his power so deeply into a tree trunk that only Siegmund will have the strength to extricate it. Wotan knows that with it in hand, Siegmund can conquer the forces of evil. But Fricka – Wotan's wife, who is ruler of family values and stanch upholder of the values of the "old gods" – is astute enough to know that if Siegmund succeeds he will have more power than she. Her *pride* is hurt. Loge is influencing her whether she likes it or not. Fricka

---

[3] That portion of the story will be detailed more in Chapter 4.

also realizes that Siegmund will not be using his own power but that of Wotan, since Wotan set it up so that Siegmund would find the sword and have use of it. It would be Wotan's power, not Siegmund's, that would be used to save humanity. In order to save humanity, and the gods, from the forces of evil a person completely independent from him and the other old gods is needed. Fricka confronts Wotan with this flaw in his logic, and he has to admit that she is right. He realizes he must remove his power from the sword. He orders his daughter Brünnhilde to do this. Brünnhilde, however, does not. Wotan learns that the power is still in the sword, and he removes the power himself. When Siegmund goes to use the sword in battle it breaks, and Siegmund is killed.

This would be the end of Wotan's story of redemption, except that Siegmund's consort, Sieglinde, is pregnant with Siegmund's child. Wotan is ignorant of this, and will remain so, but his daughter Brünnhilde knows. Brünnhilde has taken Sieglinde to a forest where Wotan never goes. Siegmund's and Sieglinde's child will be completely independent of Wotan and, therefore, have the potential to overcome the forces of evil.

Near the end of *The Valkyrie*, Wotan confronts Brünnhilde with her failure to remove his power from Siegmund's sword. Brünnhilde had willfully and intentionally acted against his command. Wotan truly loves this daughter, but he now has no choice but to disown her and cast her off. She pleads with him to show mercy. He refuses to budge. She tries everything she can think of to dissuade him. Finally she says:

> … if you sever
> the bonds that we tied,
> then half your being
> you have abandoned,
> which once belonged to you only.
> O god, forget not that!
> That other self
> you must not dishonor;
> if you disgrace her,
> it falls on you:
> your fame then would be darkened,
> if I were scorned and despised! (147)

Without a doubt she is appealing to his pride. But through and because of his anguish over his mistakes Wotan has been humbled. He has learned his lessons and has overcome his selfish pride. He will not give in to Brünnhilde. He can now work with Loge/Lucifer for higher purposes. He is in control! He has overcome Loge/Lucifer and will not fall prey again to the sin of pride.

Wotan has decided to banish Brünnhilde to the earthly plain. But rather than leave Brünnhilde in a condition that would leave her at the mercy of the first person to come across her, as he had originally intended, Wotan now agrees to protect her in such a way that only a person worthy of her can find her. He places her atop a rock and calls on Loge:

Loge, hear!
Come at my call!
As when first you were found,
a fiery glow,
as when then you escaped me,
a wandering flicker;
once you were bound:
be so again!
Arise! Come flickering Loge;
surround the rock, ring it with flame!
Loge! Loge! Appear!
Only the man
who braves my spear-point
can pass through this sea of flame! (152)

Loge is a fiery spirit, and now his flame is being used at the command of Wotan for a high purpose, which will be presented in the third *Ring Cycle* opera, *Siegfried*. In that opera, Wotan's use of Loge to encircle Brünnhilde with a flame that can only be passed through by a man who knows no fear will result in Wotan's spiritual daughter, Brünnhilde, working with his physical grandson, Siegfried, to save humanity from the forces of evil.

By mastering our lower forces, as Wotan does in *The Valkyrie*, Lucifer works with us for higher purposes! A lesson Steiner would later teach in many ways.

CHAPTER 3
WOTAN AND BRÜNNHILDE

Rudolf Steiner has gone into a lot of detail to describe the evolution of the planets, especially in the books *An Outline of Occult Science* and *Theosophy*, in which he explains how the planets divided to form other planets. The "planets" can be viewed as referring to stages of consciousness as well as to the physical planets in our solar system. In this chapter I will show how the principles of division and evolution that Steiner refers to in the two books mentioned above are reflected in Wagner's description of the spiritual beings Wotan and Brünnhilde.

The four states of consciousness that I touched on early in the first chapter of this book evolved in the following manner. What was originally a unified state of warmth divided, or went through a process of condensation, and refinement took place within that warmth. The condensed portion of that warmth was referred to as a gaseous state. That gaseous state followed a similar process, part of it refining and part of it condensing, and a fluid state resulted. The process of refinement and separation repeated, and a solid state came into existence. Our words cannot do justice to these spiritual events so we use words that represent these states of consciousness in an *analogous* sense. In esoteric language the state of warmth is called fire, the gaseous state air, the fluid state water, and the solid state earth. Earth is the occult term for the physical condition.

This process of separation and condensation is how spiritual evolution, and the evolution of human consciousness, takes place. In the spiritual world refinements and condensations occur in a way that is somewhat analogous to ores from a mine being refined into pure minerals on earth. They are crushed and/or chemically broken down into smaller pieces. When the pieces get small enough a different element is created.

In *The Ring* Brünnhilde's mother is Erda, the earth spirit (107), and her father is Wotan (100, 140 and 222). Brünnhilde and her sisters, the Valkyries, are the spirits responsible for transporting Wotan's fallen human soldiers from Earth to Valhalla, his castle in the spiritual world. Brünnhilde, though, is special; she is part of Wotan. Brünnhilde does nothing except obey her father's will (103), and Wagner tells us she actually *is his will* (106 and 112).

In order to explain the separation of Wotan and Brünnhilde I must first revisit the events that lead to it. Wotan is one of the "old gods" but unlike the other old gods Wotan is in support of humanity progressing and becoming free. He does not understand exactly what freedom is, but he knows that in order to correct his mistakes he has to make a person who is independent of the gods (101). This will not be easy. People of his era are like puppets in the hands of the gods, and that is the antithesis of freedom. The connection has to be broken, but the puppets are not prepared to survive without the gods' assistance. They first must be prepared and weaned. Wotan's wife Fricka, another of the old gods, is incensed at the thought of her slaves becoming independent. She is adamant about not wanting any of them to be free. Fricka senses that by becoming free, or independent, humanity will become superior to her. She especially does not want Wotan's illegitimate children to become free. Wotan, therefore, is alone on his quest. With no one to guide him, trial and error become the hallmarks of his effort to create a person independent of the gods.

In *The Valkyrie* Wotan arranges for his earthly son, Siegmund, to find Wotan's sword, full of Wotan's power, at a time when Siegmund will be in great peril. Wotan thinks that by defeating his enemies, *who are Fricka's slaves*, Siegmund can become independent of the gods. Fricka does not understand freedom, but she knows that Wotan is endeavoring to create a person independent of the gods. She sees the flaw in Wotan's plan and points it out to him: if Wotan's power is in the sword, it will be Wotan, *not Siegmund*, who will be defeating Siegmund's enemies. How could this be viewed as creating a person independent of the gods? Fricka makes Wotan see his error, and she demands that his power be removed from the sword.

Two points are brought out here. First, there is dissension among the gods: all is not pure harmony in the spiritual world. Second, humans (represented by Siegmund) are slaves at that point: they have no freedom. The old gods are authoritative, dictatorial, and dogmatic. They do not recognize or understand freedom. In order for humanity to evolve, and find freedom and love, humans had to separate from this state of consciousness

Wotan directs his favorite spiritual daughter, Brünnhilde, to remove his power from the sword. She, being his will, agrees to do this. But she agrees reluctantly, because she and Fricka never have gotten along well, *and* because Brünnhilde sympathizes with Siegmund. When Brünnhilde first met Siegmund she was awed by his desire for freedom and love, both of which were new concepts to her. Siegmund's deep and abiding love for his consort, Sieglinde, has deeply impressed Brünnhilde. Now her father is sending her on a mission that she knows will result in Siegmund's death. Brünnhilde does not realize that Wotan is forging a path that will lead to broader human freedom. She defies Wotan's orders and does not remove the power from the sword.

When Fricka learns that the power is still in the sword, she convinces Wotan to correct the situation. He goes to the physical plane and, just as Siegmund is about to kill his adversary, takes the power out of the sword. Siegmund is killed.

Wotan then confronts Brünnhilde with her defiance of his commandment. She explains, in a beautiful aria, that she has obeyed the commandment of her father's *heart*. Although he commanded her to remove his power from the sword, his true desire, his real will, was for Siegmund to live. Wotan's order to cause Siegmund's death was forced upon him by Fricka; therefore, it did not represent her father's real will. It was an ambiguous order, and she chose to make happen what he *really* wanted. She followed the command of his heart, not his verbal order.

Wotan is moved but not dissuaded by his daughter's argument. Brünnhilde's punishment is pronounced: she will be cast off, put into a sleep-state and left on an earthly mountain. There, she will become the property of the first person to find and waken her. In other words, Brünnhilde will become a slave; and her master might be as disreputable a person as any, and a slave to Fricka. We have already seen, in the discussion about Wotan and Loge, that Wotan then amends his daughter's punishment. He calls upon Loge and commands him to surround his sleeping daughter with a flame that can be passed through only by a hero (in spiritual terms, "an initiate"). Although she is still being banished from the spiritual plane, Wotan has now made some effort to protect Brünnhilde's divine wisdom. *The Valkyrie* ends with the placement of a sleeping Brünnhilde upon a mountaintop, encircled by Loge's flame.

The separation of Wotan and Brünnhilde in *The Valkyrie* is analogous to the process of separation and refinement that human consciousness undergoes.[4] Brünnhilde and Wotan were one. But part of Wotan,

---

[4] Steiner describes this in *Theosophy* and *An Outline of Occult Science*.

Brünnhilde, has gravitated towards humanity while the other part of Wotan has set out on a path that will move him beyond the consciousness of the old gods. Brünnhilde and Wotan then become two distinct beings.

Brünnhilde descends, not out of ignorance, laziness, fear or the desire for power, but as a result of her desire to carry out Wotan's true will (145), not his reluctant will, and to unselfishly help Siegmund (and by extension, the rest of humanity) pursue freedom and love. Through the process of her fall she will eventually unite with Siegmund's son, Siegfried, and play a part in humanity's reception of divine wisdom. Wotan ascends to higher realms where he goes on to become completely unselfish, with no trace of the pride that got him into trouble in the first place.

In order for this evolution in human freedom to occur Wotan has to release his lower consciousness, as represented in Brünnhilde, even though he loves her very much. He cannot have it both ways. At first he intends simply to abandon this part of him. Brünnhilde begs him to reconsider. She knows that whoever finds her will have use of her wisdom, another two-edged sword: an evil person would use her for her evil purposes, a good person for good purposes. Brünnhilde talks Wotan into protecting her with fire so that only an initiate ("a hero") can put her wisdom to use.

Brünnhilde knows that when she is cast off from Wotan she will remain in a sleep state until somebody awakens her. In other words, by herself she will be dormant energy. She will have to partner with someone in order to function. Her situation is similar to an esoteric belief about humanity's evolution. According to Steiner, as we were condensing out of the higher world, where we had neither individuality nor freedom, we became dormant energy waiting for someone to pick us up. Lucifer did just that, and we were his puppets, at least for awhile.

According to esoteric tradition, humans became separated from the gods first by the introduction of the physical senses, which replaced atavistic clairvoyance[5], and then by the introduction of the intellect, which further erased awareness of the spiritual world. The materialism of the last couple of centuries has nearly erased all memory of a time when humans were dependent upon gods, but it has done so at the expense of

---

[5] Atavistic clairvoyance is represented by the "old gods" in Wagner's *Ring Cycle*. Atavistic means something given to a person such as through heredity. The old clairvoyance is referred to many times by Steiner as atavistic clairvoyance. It enabled a person to "see" into the spiritual world, without physical eyes, but it was passive and not clear. In the Rhinegold we are told:

The Sunlight is greeting the gold.
Through the watery gloom
she calls to the sleeper to wake.
She kisses his eyelids,
Tells them to open. (12-13)

A new clear way of thinking is beginning, and the old atavistic clairvoyance is on its way out.

our spiritual awareness. Today we are at a point where freedom *and* spirituality are incubating, but strong opposition to freedom exists from forces that a character like Fricka best illustrates; those who want to preserve the past so that they can retain authority. They can be found in most aspects of culture worldwide today, but especially in politics and religion.

The solution is found in the problem. The intellect used for mundane purposes only, keeps us isolated from the spiritual world. But when used to understand the spiritual world it connects us with that world and brings us *consciously* into it. This was one of Steiner's core tenets: that human beings are capable of evolving to a state that allows entrance into the spiritual world in a conscious manner.

CHAPTER 4

THE GIANTS: SHADES OF CAIN AND ABLE

The biblical story of Cain and Able is one of several stories illustrating humanity's fall from grace[6]. In it, Able is a herdsman, representative of a man dependent upon God (who provides him his flocks), and Cain is a farmer, representative of a more self-reliant man (who must earn his living by the sweat of his brow). Hallmarks of their story are the slaying of Able by Cain, Cain's denial of this before God, and Cain's subsequent estrangement from God. Theirs is one of many stories that depict humanity's shift away from spiritual awareness and toward materialism. Another version of the Cain and Able story is called "The Temple Legend," which Steiner talks about in a lecture series by the same name and which I will paraphrase later in this chapter. Wagner presents his version of Cain and Able within the story of the Giants who build Valhalla.

Giants and other large creatures are often used in mythology to represent old forces which hinder evolution. In the story of Jason and the Argonauts

---

[6]The fall from grace is the process of separation, which I've discussed in Chapters 1 and 3.

his crewman Castor, the twin brother of Pollux[7], has to fight King Amycus, who is exceptionally large and represents the old forces. In *The Odyssey*, Odysseus has to overcome the huge one-eyed monster Cyclops. In the Bible, little David has to overcome the much larger and older Goliath. These stories have in common a smaller (more incarnated) person defeating a much larger foe by using their intellect, or being more cunning.

The victors in these stories demonstrate smartness and cleverness, traits that represent a developed intellect. This is something their older foes lacked. The old forces represent an earlier stage of development, which used to be good, but as Steiner has said, something good being used inappropriately at a later time is evil. The younger forces in these stories represent a more recent level of incarnation whose life force, or etheric body[8], has either condensed fully or more fully into the physical body. They have the task of proceeding where the old forces cannot go. Wagner's Giants represent the last of the early beings who once ruled the earth (206).

I will now paraphrase Rudolf Steiner's discussion of Cain and Able, which he presents at length in his lecture series "The Temple Legend." Able represents a side of humanity that had leaned toward the spiritual, and Cain represents a side that had learned toward

---

[7]Castor and Pollux are also known astrologically, as the Gemini twins.

[8] The etheric body is the spiritual force which gives life to the chemicals that make up our physical body. It is the same energy that gives plants life.

materialism. This does not make Cain bad: on the contrary, he had a necessary task to perform. In order for humanity to develop the materialistic (solid state) consciousness, which the left brain faculties support, mankind would need to master the physical world; and Cain was the leader of that era. But, as previously mentioned, in order to progress humanity had to break the old ties with its spiritual side before this could occur. In the Bible this is expressed as Cain killing Able. Very likely an actual killing did take place, but the point is the same whether it did or not. Humanity's higher, spiritual side was eliminated so that the lower, mundane side could develop.

According to Steiner, with the crucifixion of Christ the time came for those who in previous incarnations had been in the materialistic (Cain) stream to change over to the spiritual (Able) stream, and vice versa. This crossover would allow the two forces to combine and rise up to higher levels of consciousness. Of course, this could not happen automatically. It would be a gradual event and, obviously, a lot of resistance in the quest for higher consciousness still exists today. In the Giants Fasolt and Fafner, Wagner gives a very clear example of the beginning of the division between these two sides.

Wotan has contracted Fasolt and Fafner to build Valhalla, Wotan's spiritual fortress. They complete the job as specified and come to Wotan for their payment, which was to be Wotan's sister-in-law, Freia, the goddess of youth and beauty. In Scene 2 of *The Rhinegold* Fricka scolds Wotan for making such a deal. Wotan reminds her that she, too, wanted Valhalla, but he repents of his bargain with the Giants, which had been Loge's suggestion. When Fasolt and Fafner arrive to claim payment, Wotan tells them to demand some other wage; they cannot have Freia.

Fasolt warns Wotan that war will result if he fails to maintain his bargain (24). Wotan tries to talk the Giants out of the agreement, suggesting that the goddess of love and beauty can have no appeal to them (24) Fafner agrees and states that her charms mean nothing (24) but Fasolt stands firm. Fasolt (Able) wants Freia (26), but Fafner (Cain) declares that the real glory is in the gold which Alberich possesses (30).

Wagner's notation to the opera's director is that Fasolt's demeanor indicates he will reluctantly go along with Fafner's proposal. Fafner tells Wotan that the Giants will accept a lesser payment; namely, the gold (33). When Wotan questions how he is expected to get the gold Fafner replies that they, the Giants, were unable to get it from Alberich but that Wotan, with his cunning, can easily obtain it (Fafner is mistaken: it is not Wotan who is cunning, but his consultant Loge/Lucifer; but that would not have been apparent to the Giants.)

Fasolt says Freia will be their hostage in the meantime, and Fafner concurs (33). Wotan has until that evening to deliver the gold. If he does not meet that deadline, says Fasolt, Freia will be theirs forever (34).

Everything the Giants have said makes it clear that Fasolt wants the beauty and youth of Freia, while Fafner wants the gold and does not care about Freia's attributes. Wagner, with a little bit of literary license, uses Fasolt to represent the Able stream, and Fafner the Cain stream.

Loge and Wotan steal the gold back from Alberich, but in the process Alberich places a curse of death upon the gold – whoever possesses it will die. Loge wants to give the gold back to the Rhinemaidens[9] (63) but Wotan overrules him and prepares to ransom Freia.

Fasolt and Fafner return with Freia and direct Loge and Wotan to pile up the golden items until they completely block her from view. Wotan hopes to keep *the ring* for himself, but all the gold piled before Freia still leaves her eyes uncovered. The Giants demand that space be filled, (Fasolt pleading that so long as she is visible to him his love for her cannot be set aside) and Wotan has no choice but to place *the ring* on the pile, perfectly filling the space that had kept Freia's eye visible.

---

[9]The Rhinemaidens are spiritual beings and would not be impacted by the curse. If Loge had succeeded in returning the gold to the Rhinemaidens at that point, the story would have been one of consciousness reverting to a dreamlike state. Humans would have dissolved into the spiritual world with no individuality or freedom. This is an important point because it is how the lower, unredeemed Lucifer works: he wants things to return to the state that existed before the fall.

The Giants then prepare to leave; but in the process of piling the gold into their bags, Fafner decides he wants all of the gold for himself. Fasolt protests, and Fafner asserts that Fasolt never really wanted the gold; all he wanted was Freia. Without further ado, Fafner murders Fasolt and takes all the gold for himself. This is Cain killing Able.

Wotan realizes the power of Alberich's curse and Loge reminds him how lucky he was to have given up *the ring* (68).

Fafner reappears in Act 2, Scene 1 of the third opera, *Siegfried*. Siegmund's son, Siegfried, is young, strong, smart, more than a little egotistical, and fearless. As one of Siegfried's initiation trials he has to slay "the dragon." The dragon is symbolic of our lower nature and instincts. In Wagner's *Ring* it just so happens that the dragon is Fafner, the Giant. After killing Fasolt and taking all the gold Fafner moves into a cave, where he can hoard the gold and make sure no one steals it from him. By the time we meet him again, Fafner has transformed into a dragon.

Alberich is camping outside the cave trying to connive a way to steal the gold from Fafner. Alberich realizes that due to his curse of death on the gold, the dragon must die (194), and he wants to be there when that happens, so he can get the gold.

Wotan appears at the entrance to the cave. He is now known as the Wanderer. The fact that he has a new name is symbolic of him having risen to higher stages of initiation. He has passed his tests and has gone from being the leader of the "old" gods to being a "traveler" who is concerned with larger and higher realms. In esoteric terms, a guardian angel is responsible for one person, and an angel who influences a certain territory and its people is known as an archangel.[10] The third and highest realm of angels is known as the archai.[11] In esoteric terms, by the third opera, *Siegfried*, Wotan is ascending to a realm analogous to that of the archai.[12]

Wotan's task is to guide humanity to a consciousness of freedom and love. His first effort toward fulfillment of that task had been aimed at preparing Siegmund for victory in battle. Although Wotan's way of doing that was a mistake, it was the beginning. A certain amount of trial and error is inevitable. The Wanderer knows that Siegfried, whose life is intertwined with the drama set in motion by Wotan's early mistakes, will do battle with the dragon. The Wanderer confronts Alberich and assures him he will not interfere. If he were to do so Siegfried would not be able to become free, and forwarding humanity's freedom is the Wanderer's task.

---

[10]Further reading: *The Spiritual Hierarchies: Their Reflection in the Physical World* by Rudolf Steiner (available online in a text format.)

[11] The archai are associated with long periods of time, each period having a specific and unique purpose related to the development of consciousness An introduction to the structure of these time periods can be found in the sidebar below.

[12] In so doing, Wotan's relationships dramatically shift. No longer will he be active as husband to Fricka, or father to his children, or leader to his warriors. His time for ruling territory and people is passing.

However, the Wanderer reminds Alberich that Siegfried will be there to take *the ring* from Fafner, and then tells Alberich that since Siegfried is innocent he will not be affected by Alberich's curse.

The Wanderer then calls Fafner and awakens him.

In the meantime Alberich's brother, Mime, has lured Siegfried into fighting the dragon by explaining to him that it is the only way to learn fear, something Siegfried has no knowledge of and desperately wants to experience. Mime knows that Siegfried's fate is tied to the gold stolen from the Rhinemaidens so many years before, and he has raised Siegfried from birth with the intention of getting that gold for himself. Now that Siegfried has proven himself ready (through the re-forging of his father's sword[13]) Mime presents Siegfried with the task of learning fear via a battle with the dragon. Mime hopes that both the dragon and Siegfried will be killed, allowing him to take the gold for himself.

Fafner in the form of the dragon represents what Steiner calls the Guardian of the Threshold, a creature that Steiner discusses in many books and lectures. Its function is to make sure we do not cross into the spiritual world prematurely. If we were to do so we would

---

[13] Siegfried does not know who his father was: Mime has kept him in the dark about his parentage. Mime has been trying to re-forge Siegmund's shattered sword for many years; however, his methods cannot overcome the weapon's weakness where the breaks occurred. Finally, Siegfried takes the broken pieces from Mime and re-forges them in a way that demonstrates his difference in consciousness and makes the sword entirely his own.

be unprepared and unable to deal with adversarial spirits on the other side. This spiritual being has been created out of our negative thoughts and deeds, even those from earlier incarnations. It resembles a snake or dragon but becomes less reprehensible as we become more moral. The idea is to face up to this beast and transform it so that it can assist us in our quest for higher consciousness. We are not to run from it or, even worse, kill it.

Siegfried, however, is unaware of this possibility in the dragon. Although his lineage (of which he is unaware) makes him full of potential, at this point Siegfried is a misled hero with several spiritual weaknesses. Like his spiritual grandfather, he will make many mistakes along the pathway of his task.[14]

Siegfried takes his sword and travels to the dragon's cave. Fafner awakens. He and Siegfried have a robust fight, after which Siegfried realizes that the dragon may be able to tell him the identity of his father. Siegfried asks the dragon, but it is too late. Fafner dies before he can enlighten Siegfried. Siegfried must find out about his father, and himself, in some other way.

Because Siegfried killed the dragon he was left without a helper who might have taught him about both his earthly father (Siegmund) and his spiritual grandfather (Wotan). If Siegfried had tamed the dragon, he would have known something of his physical and spiritual ancestry. He might have realized his divine nature then,

---

[14] It is Siegfried's lower nature that Hitler tended to praise.

and become properly prepared to meet Brünnhilde. As it is, his battle with the dragon has not advanced his spiritual awareness. Siegfried still has not experienced fear, but he soon will. That event will usher in The *Twilight of the Gods*.

Sidebar: The time period associated with major transitions in the evolution of human consciousness is called a Great Month, and is equal to 2,160 years. This is one-twelfth of the time it takes Earth to complete the precession of the equinoxes. Our sun passes over Earth's equator at a slightly different longitude each year. Not by much, but after 25,920 years it returns to the same spot on the equator. This is known as a Great Year, and one twelfth of that is 2,160 years, a.k.a. a Great Month. One-seventh of 2,160 is a little over 300 years, and that is the length of time the various leading archai take turns ruling. In our year 2011, Michael (formerly known as Michael the Archangel) is the ruling archai.

CHAPTER 5

THE FIRST THREE CULTURAL EPOCHS:

8227 BCE TO 747 BCE

Rudolf Steiner lectured and wrote extensively on what he calls the seven cultural epochs of earthly evolution. Each of these epochs represents a unique time in the development of human consciousness and is approximately 2,160 years in length. A cultural epoch is often referred to as a Great Month, and each Great Month is one-twelfth the precession of the equinoxes, or one-twelfth of the 25,920 years it takes for the sun to return to any given point on Earth's equator.[15] How does this tie to human consciousness? According to Steiner and esoteric belief systems, the stars are not merely balls of gas in the heavens. *Everything is spirit, and stars are spiritual beings.* Each has its unique influence which affects us on Earth. The nature of a star's influence increases, decreases, or changes in other ways as its *position* changes relative to Earth and also to other spiritual bodies.[16]

---

[15] The precession is caused by the fact that the sun crosses Earth's equator at a slightly different longitude each year. It will take 25,920 years for the sun to cross again at exactly the same equatorial location.

[16] The spiritual beings that we perceive as stars guide, or impel, human beings. This is the significance of the cultural epochs. Fear not: this does not even come close to meaning that we do not have free will. Humans are endowed with free will, though people who

Astronomically speaking the first of these seven 2,160-year cycles began in 8227 BCE in the sign of Cancer the Crab, the second in 5067 BCE in the sign of Gemini the Twins, the third in 2907 BCE in the sign of Taurus the Bull, and the fourth in 747 BCE, in Aries the Ram. The present epoch, the fifth, began in 1413 CE in Pisces the Fish, and the sixth, the Age of Aquarius, will begin in 3573. Sometimes there is speculation or quibbling over the *exact* number of years and the precise time at which a transition begins, but for the purposes of this topic what is important is the larger idea: that a transition in consciousness *does* take place in coordination with the motion of heavenly bodies. These dates may vary a little and even then they are very controversial. Those who try to define the dates by scientific data alone are left with many questions including when to start the clock; however, these dates do coincide with historical events from the third epoch on. The predominant use of bulls in art during the third (Taurus) period, rams (Aries) in the fourth, and fish (Pisces) in the fifth period is notable. The third

---

are limited to lower consciousness are often slaves to their emotions and feelings, and as a result are easily manipulated by those who take advantage of their lower state of consciousness. But as we develop our higher consciousness we gradually become freer. Spiritual beings do not compel people operating from higher consciousness to do anything. However, the closer we follow the path which they are impelling us to take the more freedom, love, and creative capacity we develop. How we make use of their guidance is up to us. In the epilogue I will discuss how forces counter to evolution use principles touched upon here in ways counter to the ideals of freedom: those forces want their idea of god to control the masses so as to deprive humanity of freedom.

cycle coincides with the rise of the great Egyptian and other Middle Eastern civilizations, the fourth with the rise of the Greek philosophers and the Jewish prophets, and the fifth with the Renaissance.

Wagner's first *Ring Cycle* opera, *The Rhinegold*, takes place during the first and second of these seven cultural epochs. The first had to do with humanity's "fall," and the second cultural epoch had to do with the duality of Lucifer and Ahriman, which is discussed in Chapter 1. Not coincidentally, the precession of the equinoxes at that time was in Gemini, the sign of the twins.

During the *first* 2,160-year cycle human beings were so different from what we are today that we do not have a frame of reference to compare ourselves to them. The important aspect of the time was that people thought of the spiritual world as their true home as they came down to Earth, so to speak. The way I choose to describe the "fall" is that it began when people's consciousness started to see "parts" and "pieces" rather than the oneness or unity of the spiritual world. Mankind began to see the trees rather than the forest. Keeping in mind that the "fall" is an ongoing process that in some ways is still occurring, this was the period in which the view, or consciousness, of the "whole" *began* to be obliterated. In other words, atavistic clairvoyance was coming to an end. Materialism was beginning. I define *materialism* as consciousness of the physical world – that is, the world of parts and pieces which appear to be solid and separate – without awareness of the spiritual world. They experienced the transition and time on Earth as what we would call an altered state of consciousness. Wagner portrays this transition period as golden haze transforming into a clear light as it solidifies into the element gold. Alberich (Ahriman) leads the way into materialism when he perceives gold as a physical substance rather than universal (or divine) wisdom, which is spiritual. Wagner borrowed from Nordic mythology to tell this part of his story, and he gives Wotan one eye, which in mythology symbolizes the *old* form of clairvoyance; or atavistic clairvoyance. The old clairvoyance was diminishing during the previous periods, but the major turning point would come in the third 2,160-year cycle.

The second *Ring Cycle* opera, *The Valkyrie*, takes place in the third cultural epoch. According to Steiner, prior to this epoch clairvoyance was the norm, and indeed, Greek literature is full of stories about the ancients observing the gods and often having their fates determined by the gods. At that point in the development of human freedom, the conditions for human freedom did not exist. The first two epochs were the time when gods and goddesses like Fricka loomed large. In order for human freedom as we know it to blossom, higher levels of consciousness had to take develop.

The spiritual beings that we perceive as stars guide, or impel, human beings. Humans are endowed with free will, though people who are limited to lower consciousness are often slaves to their emotions and feelings, and as a result are easily manipulated by those who take advantage of their lower state of consciousness. But as we develop our higher consciousness we gradually become freer. Spiritual beings do not compel people operating from higher consciousness to do anything. However, the closer we follow the path which they are impelling us to take the more freedom, love, and creative capacity we develop. How we make use of their guidance is up to us.

What differentiates the third cultural epoch from the previous two is the development of mankind's physical senses. Prior to the third cultural epoch, humans did not hear, see, feel, smell or taste in the ways we do now. The widespread power of atavistic clairvoyance meant the physical senses as we now know them were *not necessary for perception*. But in the third cultural epoch humanity was being prepared for greater independence from the gods, and development of the physical senses *was* necessary. Without these tools to replace the atavistic clairvoyance that was rapidly ending, humanity would have died out. Mankind's physical senses represent the next step in the evolution of human consciousness and freedom.

In *The Valkyrie*, which is allegorically set in the third cultural epoch, we hear Sieglinde sing:

My heart felt the spell,
grew warm when you came;
when my eyes beheld you, I knew you. (91)

She *felt* the spell; her heart *grew warm*; she *knew* when her eyes beheld him. Her knowledge came through physical sensations, and the love that results is necessary in the unfolding story of human freedom from the gods.

In spite of the budding independence from the gods and the spiritual world which the senses provided, in the third cultural epoch there still was no individuality within humanity's consciousness. People did not feel themselves part of the spiritual world anymore, but neither had individual egos been established. They felt themselves to be part of a race, tribe, family, or some other kind of a group. To be cast out meant death. In a short while, we'll see how Wagner uses the loss of a family to show a more individual consciousness beginning to form within the characters of Siegmund and Sieglinde, the human heroes of the second opera.

Just as there was no individuality, there was no freedom during the third cultural epoch. People could not overpower their emotions, and their emotions were controllable only through their senses. Intellectual consciousness had not yet developed. People could also be manipulated by *others* through their emotions. One of the basic ways of doing this would be for someone (perhaps a military ruler, a religious leader, or a town bully) to instill fear in a person in order to make that person submissive. Hurting a person – whether by twisting their arm, burning their crops, or threatening them with eternal damnation – would be a way to manipulate them, using their emotional responses to get them to toe the line. This is still the case today, thousands of years later, except that as evolution progresses more and more people are gaining control over their emotions.

The second *Ring Cycle* opera, *The Valkyrie*, describes the struggle of the leading edge of humanity as they try to develop individuality and freedom. It takes place near the end of the third cultural epoch, when humanity was trying to break free of its subservience to the gods so as to develop freedom and love.

The Valkyrie opens with a stormy prelude played by the orchestra. Siegmund, completely exhausted and looking like a fugitive, enters a stranger's house (In German the prefix "Sieg" means initiate.) Sieglinde comes to his aid. He tells her he had to flee his enemies because his shield and spear were not as strong as his body. This is allegorical-speak for his spiritual defenses (consciousness) being inadequate to compete with his adversaries. It is common in mythology to use the terms shield and sword when referring to spiritual defenses.

Hunding was Sieglinde's husband, and the person whom Siegmund had been fighting. Yet when Hunding comes home he and Siegmund do not recognize each other. Siegmund tells them his name is Wehwalt, which means sorrow. Hunding senses there is something between his wife and Siegmund. Siegmund tells them of the time he and his father returned home after being chased by their foes only to find their home ruined, an oak tree reduced to a stump, his mother dead, and his sister missing (83). The allegories continue: "home" would refer to the family. It is symbolic of what Siegmund's family used to be, not just a house. Their family has been destroyed. The oak tree is an extremely strong and durable tree: it signifies what the family used to be but is no longer. In mythology the feminine, in this case his mother and sister, represent the soul forces, those inner qualities which have to do with feelings. Siegmund and his father managed to survive the many attacks on them but, eventually, they became separated. In mythology the masculine, in this case the father, would represent spiritual qualities that apply universally. Siegmund had no friends; what he thought was right, others thought was wrong, and vice-versa. Their past was over. Wagner has given us a pictorial, mythological description of the fall from paradise, and has begun to sketch Siegmund as an individual — an identity able to survive separate from tribe or family.

Later, Siegmund tells of trying to save a maiden from a forced marriage to a person she feared. He failed and thought she was killed. This maiden turns out to be Sieglinde. Hunding senses that there is a connection between Sieglinde and Siegmund, and realizes that his guest is his enemy. He declares that he will allow Siegmund to stay in his house for the night but tomorrow they fight to the death. Hunding goes to bed, and Sieglinde drugs him into a deep sleep. Siegmund and she talk. She tells him of her enslavement and abuse. He tells of his father having put a sword into the trunk of an oak tree so that he would have it in the moment of greatest need. The sword is an allegory for the power of his father (higher spiritual forces).

Sieglinde now senses and realizes Siegmund is her brother. She takes him to the tree trunk, and shows him Wotan's sword embedded there. Siegmund does what Hunding and his cronies have been unable to do: he pulls the sword out of the tree. It now belongs to him. He and Sieglinde know without a doubt that he will be the victor the following morning. They have fallen in love.

The love that Siegmund and Sieglinde are experiencing in this scene reveals a new aspect of consciousness, which involves freely uniting with another person. Humanity would have to develop this capability, in spite of massive opposition. The old forces did not believe in love nor did they want its attributes to exist among humanity. They wanted to be in control, and they would often fight to the death for that control, or manipulate others to fight for them. At one time lack of freedom and desire for control were not only reasonable but necessary, since people were not mature enough to manage on their own … but times change. Siegmund and Sieglinde represent the leaders of humanity at that time, pursuing freedom and love.

The thought of brother and sister making physical love has turned a lot of people away from this opera; however, in mythology such a pairing is not uncommon. In the spiritual world there is no such thing as incest, and there are no genetic consequences. On the physical level Sieglinde and Siegmund are brother and

sister[17], but allegorically and esoterically Sieglinde and
Siegmund are on a spiritual level where incest does not
exist.

Wagner now takes the battle to the next level, that
of the gods.

Fricka, Wotan's wife, is the old god who is the ruler of marriages (98). She is aware that Siegmund and
Sieglinde have committed adultery and she has taken it
as an injury to both her servant, Hunding, and herself.
She demands that Wotan put a stop to it. Wotan says
he considers "vows that bind unloving hearts" to be unholy. Fricka condemns their incest, which she perceives
because she looks down on them as purely physical beings: she cannot see them on a spiritual plane. Wotan
says she is concerned with the past, he with the future
(100), and then he tells her that in order for the gods to
be saved a person who is free from the gods is necessary.
Only such a person can do what the old gods could not
do for themselves. What could this possibly mean?

First, his comment on her being concerned with
the past and he being concerned with the future. In
Chapter 3 the principle of refinement and condensation in regards to evolution was discussed. This applies
to the old gods, too. When Lucifer fell he took us with
him. But we were part of the whole at that time. In
other words we were a part of the old gods. We fell
into lower stages of consciousness. The principle of

_____

[17] The libretto says that Wotan is their father and their mother is a
"common woman" (100).

refinement and condensation applies here. Wotan rises to higher levels, while Fricka and many of the other old gods fall or remain behind at their previous level. There are lessons that can be learned on Earth that cannot be learned in the higher spiritual worlds, so a great deal of good can come out of all this. On Earth, we can observe parts and pieces and use deductive (intellectual, analytical) reasoning to put them together. Clear understanding and creativity can occur, and the development of those faculties can prepare us for a return to the spiritual plane in a conscious state. This is what *The Ring* about: clear understanding being developed so that a higher stage of consciousness, freedom and love can arise.

Now for Wotan's second comment, that without a free human being the gods will be lost. Remember that in the process of separation and condensation, the two entities begin as one. Upon separation, the entity that rises and the entity that falls go on to new and necessary tasks; one higher, one lower. When we were cast out of paradise, we took a part of the gods with us. Their task changed, and our task changed, but the two entities were still in service to a common higher goal. The gods needed us to accomplish our task (freedom) in order for them to accomplish their task and move on to higher realms. They needed us to succeed for our sake and for theirs. Wotan is telling his wife that if they prevent humanity from evolving, they too will die out. They *need* a human to be free from the gods. Without that independence, the candidate cannot lead humanity to the next level and the old gods will be doomed (101).

This makes no sense whatsoever to Fricka. She accuses Wotan of attempting to trick her with "crafty reasoning" and "new excuses," and remains committed to the old ways. Fricka knows that Wotan has arranged Siegmund's victory over Hunding by putting the sword in the tree trunk with Wotan's power intact. Fricka sets Wotan straight: as long as Wotan's power is in the sword, Siegmund cannot be operating free from the gods. She is right, and the consequences are that the opera closes with humanity still enslaved to the gods; however, there is hope. Wotan takes the power out of the sword. It shatters during the fight, and Hunding kills Siegmund. But Sieglinde is pregnant, and Brünnhilde has hustled Sieglinde away from Wotan (125). Their son, Siegfried, will be on his own. Hopefully, Siegfried, in the fourth cultural epoch can find the freedom and love that Wotan and Siegmund do not find in the third cultural epoch.

Steiner tells many times of the need for the human race to lose its old, atavistic clairvoyance in order to proceed to the next step in earthy evolution. It is not that clairvoyance is bad, it is the type of clairvoyance and the time frame that weaken its value in human evolution. The old atavistic clairvoyance was a necessary part of life in the early stages of evolution. But to keep it would be to prevent progress. The old clairvoyance had to go so that a higher form of clairvoyance could be created, one that included clear understanding and free will. Steiner taught that humanity had to lose its ancient clairvoyance. Wagner made the same point by creating Wotan, whose single eye means he is from the era of atavistic clairvoyance, and who realizes that for his own redemption he must create a man who is free from dependence upon the gods.

CHAPTER 6

THE FOURTH CULTURAL EPOCH: 747 CE AND THE INTELLECT

The third opera in *The Ring Cycle* is *Siegfried*, presents an allegory that spans the fourth and fifth cultural epochs. In this chapter I will focus on *Siegfried* as an allegory of the fourth cultural epoch. This opera focuses on the character of Siegfried, the son of Sieglinde and Siegmund. On an esoteric level it is about how the leading initiates of the time, represented in composite as this opera's title character, took human consciousness to a new level, and about the obstacles that their progress encountered.

In *The Valkyrie*, the representatives of the leading initiates failed because they were attempting to accomplish in the third cultural epoch what could only be done in the fourth. They failed in one sense but in another way they succeeded, because preliminary steps had to be taken and those they took. Siegfried was conceived and Wotan finally learned what it meant to not interfere with humanity's quest for freedom.

Rudolf Steiner calls the fourth cultural epoch the Age of the Intellectual Soul. This was when rational, intellectual, analytical thinking, as we know it, developed in mankind. Historically speaking it took place at the time the Greek philosophers and the Jewish prophets came on the scene. The astronomical date that it began is 747 BCE, but it must be remembered that these transitions are gradual. Events prior to that date led up to it and its development took over 2,000 years. In some ways it is still in progress, and in some ways the intellectual soul has run beyond a healthy level and limits our consciousness to the physical, mechanical world. The fourth cultural epoch ended in 1413 CE, astronomically speaking, at which time humanity was to begin rising up to a higher consciousness of the spiritual world. In *Siegfried*, Richard Wagner gives us a mythological look at the fourth epoch, resistance to the accomplishment of its purpose, and its limitations.

In the third cultural epoch the physical senses came into being. Humanity accomplished many things, including irrigation techniques and the building of the pyramids. People could learn without the intellect but their accomplishments were limited to what they could learn by imitation, trial and error to a certain extent, and from inspiration from the gods. As populations increased people spread out to new lands in order to have enough food. These new areas were not as simple to cultivate as were the first areas and at some point the intellect was needed in order to come up with the technology necessary for advanced irrigation, agriculture, animal husbandry, etc. Jared Diamond goes into this in his Pulitzer Prize winning book *Guns, Germs and Steel.* He does not mention, and probably does not believe in, new stages of consciousness that were associated with the 2,160-year cycles. He limits advances in technology to an inevitable mechanical process. Although he omitted the spiritual aspect of the evolution of human thinking I learned a great deal from his book. Wagner's mythological operas cannot explain the details of the changes brought about in the fourth cultural epoch as Diamond and Steiner do, but he does give us an artistic picture of the struggle to take humanity to a higher level of consciousness.

In *Siegfried*, we learn that Sieglinde died giving birth to Siegfried. He was raised in isolation, deep in the woods, by Mime, the evil brother of Alberich. Mime had an ulterior motive for this: he had the fragments of Siegmund's sword and if he could re-forge the sword he could manipulate Siegfried into using it to kill Fafner, the dragon. Mime could then kill Siegfried, and abscond with the gold. However, although Mimi was a highly skilled blacksmith, he could not re-forge the pieces of Siegmund's sword.

Siegfried has never known a guardian other than Mime, but by observing birds, deer, foxes, and wolves he knows that all animals have two parents. Siegfried asks Mime about his mother. Mime says that *he* is both Siegfried's mother and Siegfried's father. Siegfried calls him a liar, and then explains that he knows Mime is lying because all animals look like their parents. Siegfried saw his reflection in a stream, and it was obvious that there was no resemblance between him and Mime. Siegfried's reasoning is an example of pure deductive logic:

All animals look like their parents:
I do not look like you:
Therefore, you are not my parent. (163)

This type of thinking was not available in the third cultural epoch. A close examination of the dialogues in the previous operas reveals that they used the term "feel" and not "think." Intellectual, analytical thinking was a new level of consciousness that came into being in the fourth cultural epoch. It was a big step forward in the quest to find freedom and love.

Steiner refers to the third cultural epoch as the Sentient Soul Age. Consciousness was limited to feelings which were produced through the physical senses. People were slaves to their feelings and desires, and the persons or spiritual beings who could manipulate their feelings and desires could control them. Today, in the fifth cultural epoch most people are still working on gaining a greater command of their feelings. It is not a black and white issue; there many degrees of control. Reasoning is a prerequisite for freedom, without it others can manipulate and control us through our feelings and emotions, particularly the emotion of fear, which is associated with the senses and will be discussed at length later. This issue of control is still a big factor in life today.

Siegfried tolerates Mime because he knows it is only he who can tell him about his mother. This is an allegorical statement. Siegfried not only wants to know who his physical mother is, he wants to know about his spiritual mother (soul). Mime cannot answer the second question, and he resists answering the first. Siegfried grabs him by the throat and intimidates his reluctant foster father into telling him about his mother. Mime reveals that his mother died giving birth to him. Siegfried next wants to know who his father was, but Mime only knows that he died in battle (168). Siegfried wants proof, and Mime shows him the fragments of the sword. Siegfried knows the sword will bring him freedom from Mime, so he commands him to forge the sword for him. Mime contemplates how he can get Siegfried to kill the dragon for him so that he can gain possession of *The Ring*.

This is not a subject to take lightly. It is a micro-example of the struggle between the forces of good and evil in the evolution of consciousness. Mime understands the power of *the ring* but he does not have the ability to acquire it. Siegfried does not understand it but he does have the potential to acquire it. So Mime contemplates how he can manipulate Siegfried into getting *the ring* for him. Since Siegfried is ignorant of *the ring's* power he will not be on guard to protect it. The theme we must consider at greater length is the manipulation of good people to serve evil.

At the present moment in evolution this is a crucial issue as various political, religious and cultural leaders strive to discretely manipulate good people into unwittingly turning over their higher powers to them, so that they can have control. Wagner will continue to express this theme in the rest of *The Ring*, especially in *Twilight of the Gods* and *Parsifal*, which is a standalone opera but thematically completes *The Ring Cycle*. To paraphrase Steiner, what the forces of good must do is understand the spiritual world and the struggles behind the scenes. Humanity now has the ability to do this. People must recognize evil; then work within it without becoming one with it; and without using force or deceit, transform evil into good. No small task! Wagner will not present us with the success of this until we get to *Parsifal*, but in *The Ring* he will show us, artistically, what has happened in the past and what is going on in the present epoch.

Siegfried represents the initiates who took humanity into the fourth cultural epoch. After realizing Mime is incapable of re-forging the sword Siegfried takes it upon himself to re-forge it. He files it down into extremely fine particles and then starts from scratch. Siegfried knows that it will not do to just weld the pieces together as Mime had tried to do. The raw materials have been given to him, but he must now make it his own.

CHAPTER 7
THE FIFTH CULTURAL EPOCH:
1413 CE AND THE PRESENT ERA

Steiner calls the third cultural epoch the Age of the Sentient Soul. It was the time mankind began to depend more upon the physical senses than upon clairvoyance. He calls the fourth cultural epoch the Age of the Intellectual Soul. It was the time analytical reasoning arose. He calls the fifth cultural epoch, which began astronomically speaking in 1413 CE, the Age of the Consciousness Soul.

This fifth cultural epoch is the 2,160-year period in which human consciousness should extend to the spiritual world. That is, during this time period mankind should develop the ability to consciously enter the spiritual plane. Two problems are: (1) that it represents a new dimension in consciousness that is naturally difficult for many to realize, as is the case with Siegfried, and, (2) there are strong forces which want to keep the rest of humanity ignorant of their divine nature so that they can steal their power. *Twilight of the Gods* and *Parsifal* are about this second problem.

Forces counter to humanity's spiritual progress try to work secretly through all aspects of culture. Those in opposition to the evolution of freedom and love need secrecy. When they and their methods are discovered they become impotent, which brings to mind the Biblical phrase, "The truth shall set you free." I find it encouraging that secrets have become more difficult to keep. Beginning at the end of the twentieth century and on the physical plane, the computer has done a lot to make information more widely available. On the spiritual level the consciousness of many people is rising up to spiritual levels. But old forces are still at work, opposing freedom and awareness in their efforts to regain power. Such forces prefer for humanity to be in a state of hopelessness or distraction. Rudolf Steiner has said our task in this epoch is to see and understand what is going on. I will assert that helping the forces counter to the development of human consciousness are tools such as television shows that lull people to sleep; video games that may sharpen people's reactions but bypass their reasoning; and drugs. Our task is to not kill the enemy but to transform it, and these three areas present a vast platform for initiates conscious enough to address them.

Siegfried can see into the spiritual world, but he remains blind as to the spiritual nature of what he sees. The struggle the philosophers had during the Age of Reason is similar to this, and the expression "God is dead," is an eventual outcome. The initiates represented allegorically as Siegfried took human consciousness to new and higher levels, but they could only go so far.

In the opera *Siegfried*, Siegfried's tests (adventures, as they are called in mythology) demonstrate the limitations humanity experienced during the fourth cultural epoch and which extended into the fifth. Specifically, humanity did not have the ability to fully enter into the spiritual world in a conscious state, but the time for entering in a trance was passing. The leading initiates of the fourth and early fifth cultural epoch, all of which can be allegorically related to Siegfried, had to find their way by trial and error. They had no one to show them the way. Wagner makes a strong point of this by stressing the fact that Wotan had to abandon his children if freedom and love were to become part of human consciousness. As much as he wanted to, Wotan could not do it for them nor let them do it through him. They had to do it on their own or they would not be free. It was inevitable that the conglomerate of leading initiates Siegfried represents would have failures along the way.

In Chapter 6, we saw how Siegfried demonstrates the rationalistic and intellectual abilities that had to be developed in the fourth cultural epoch. In this chapter, we will look at how humanity of the present (fifth) cultural epoch, has to use those abilities to reach higher stages of consciousness (i.e. entrance to the spiritual world in full consciousness). The goal is not to enter the spiritual world in an unconscious state (which would be akin to going back to our consciousness before the fall), but to enter the spiritual world as conscious beings, fully aware that we are entering the spiritual realm and equipped to understand what we experience in it. Again, this is a departure from the experiences of initiates in the fourth cultural epoch. Siegfried will enter the spiritual realm, but he will not realize what he has accomplished. He will not realize that he has left the physical realm and entered the spiritual realm. This will leave him open to manipulation by forces of opposition.

Siegfried's first test has already been passed. He has rejected his immoral stepfather and strives to find love as he has learned it from the animals, which he has seen caring for their young. He is seeking information about his true mother and father, or in esoteric terms his true and spiritual nature. His next test will involve facing the Guardian of the Threshold.

As discussed briefly in Chapter 4, in esoteric literature the dragon often represents the Guardian of the Threshold. Steiner has discussed this many times. The Guardian of the Threshold is a non-physical creature we have created out of our negative thoughts. Its function is to protect us from prematurely entering the spiritual world. If we were to enter the spiritual world too soon we would encounter evil spirits who would be stronger than us and able to use us for their decadent purposes. Since we start off on a low level in life the Guardian normally appears in the form of a snake, or especially in the past, as a dragon. We have to face up to this creation of ours and tame it. Wagner's version of the Guardian of the Threshold is the dragon that Fafner becomes after he killed his more spiritual brother over gold, and went off to a cave to hoard his treasure.

Siegfried knows there is a dragon because Mime tells him about it. Mime could not defeat the dragon himself so he tries to manipulate Siegfried into killing it for him so that he, Mime, can get the gold and its power to rule the world. Since Mime cannot find any other weakness he takes advantage of Siegfried's strength, his fearlessness, to manipulate him. Fear becomes an important aspect of *The Ring* and it will be explored in greater detail in Chapter 8. Siegfried falls right into Mime's scheme: he can't wait to learn this new thing called fear! It is something about which he has no conception. His curiosity is too much, and he begs Mime to teach him about fear. Mime tells him he will have to go to Fafner the dragon to learn this lesson.

Siegfried says he will visit the dragon, but he insists that Mime first re-forge his father's sword for him. Mime is a master blacksmith, but it is beyond his ability: only one who does not know fear can re-forge Siegmund's sword. Mime tries and tries again, but he cannot re-forge the sword. Mime has never failed before at metal work, and Siegfried accuses him of stalling. Siegfried then takes matters into his own hands. He begins grinding the fragments of the sword into fine particles. Mime tries to stop him because Mime's frame of reference is limited to repairing the old: he is afraid that if Siegfried continues grinding down the sword, it will be impossible to weld the pieces together again. Siegfried responds that the fragments must be "splintered and ground into shreds" (183). He is right, and he successfully re-forges the sword. Wagner is telling us that in order to move on to the next stage of consciousness we must start with the very basics, no shortcuts, and forge our own shield and spear (awareness). Soldering together the fragments of the old sword would be akin to relying on the old gods, or using Wotan's forces. By filing it down into fine shavings Siegfried is using what the gods have given him but making a new sword that is his own.

Steiner explains that before the crucifixion of Christ we were led by other spirits without our having any free will. At that time, humanity was given what it needed for survival. But things changed after what Steiner refers to as The Mystery of Golgotha. We had to fend for ourselves. Higher spirits could impel, but they would not compel us to do anything. The natural resources which were given to us would start to be depleted. We would have to take the responsibility of maintaining both ourselves and planet Earth. The higher spirits have not abandoned us, but we have to rise to higher levels of consciousness in order to find new ways of working with them.[18]

With his new sword in hand, Siegfried follows Mime toward the dragon's cave. Mime uses his wits to come up with a plan to get the gold and *the ring*. After Siegfried kills the dragon and returns to him for refreshment, Mime will poison Siegfried. Mime is on a quest for lower consciousness, that of gaining the gold and its earthly power. Siegfried is on a quest for higher consciousness, to learn about his mother and father

---

[18] Steiner's lectures on this subject are published under the same name, *The Mystery of Golgotha*.

(202). Siegfried and Mime part: Mime to wait for him by a stream, Siegfried to find the dragon.

Siegfried sees a bird (woodbird) and wishes he could understand its lovely song. He imitates its sound on a reed so that they can communicate, but he fails. Imitating the bird on a reed is symbolic of communication on a higher level. This does not work, so he tries his horn; symbolically a lower level or octave. This works, but instead of communicating with the bird he communicates with the dragon. Fafner speaks, and Siegfried can understand him. Siegfried asks the dragon to teach him about fear. Fafner thinks Siegfried will make a tasty meal. In a fight that opera directors have a great time choreographing, Siegfried mortally wounds the dragon with his sword. The dying dragon asks to know the identity of this youthful hero that has won their fight, briefly tells Siegfried who he was before he transformed into a dragon, and then warns the "hero" that the one who sent him is waiting to kill him. Siegfried senses that the dying beast has access to universal wisdom. He asks Fafner to tell him about his father, and tells the dragon his name. The dragon simply repeats Siegfried's name, and expires (206-07).

Siegfried, leading the way for humanity, had no one to tell him that the dragon should not have been killed. Had the dragon been merely subdued he would have helped Siegfried on his spiritual journey. Unfortunately, Siegfried has been manipulated by a lower force into slaying this Guardian of the Threshold. Siegfried still does not know fear, and even though he has crossed a threshold he remains unprepared for the spiritual world. Wagner has given us an example of an improper initiation into the spiritual world.[19] The rest of *The Ring* is about some of the consequences that arise from entering the spiritual world, uninitiated.

Siegfried, now operating on a higher spiritual level, clairaudiently hears the voice of the woodbird, but he still thinks he is having a physical experience. He now understands what the bird says. It tells him of the gold hoarded within the cave and that it is now his. In addition to the gold there is the tarnhelm – the magic helmet Mime forged for his brother Alberich – which enables a person to change appearances or even become invisible. There is also *the ring*, the woodbird tells him, which will make him lord of the world. Siegfried takes the tarnhelm and *the ring* but leaves the rest of the gold. Esoterically speaking gold is universal wisdom. Siegfried, having passed improperly by the Guardian of the Threshold does not realize this; he thinks of the gold as a mineral that is not important to him.

Siegfried's ability to understand the woodbird signifies that Siegfried, having passed by the Guardian of the Threshold/dragon, has reached higher levels of consciousness and is now clairaudient. Siegfried now hears what Mime *means*, not what his words say (212). He encounters Mime, who knows that Siegfried has killed the dragon and who asks whether he has experienced

---

[19] Improper initiation into the spiritual world is not all that unusual. The most common way it occurs today is through the use of drugs.

fear. Siegfried says he has not. Mime prepares the poison so he can get the treasure. He tells Siegfried that he has a refreshing drink, but Siegfried clairaudiently hears Mime say he is going to kill him and steal the gold. Mime cannot understand how Siegfried knows his thoughts, and reveals even more about his ill intentions. Siegfried has heard all he needs to hear, and with one blow of his sword kills Mime. He takes Mime's body and throws it into the cave with the gold. He then drags the dragon's body across the cave's entrance.

> The glittering gold
> you now can share
> with your foe who longed for its gleam;
> and so you both have found your rest! (216)

Siegfried has been continuously looking for someone who could guide and teach him, but without success. He now asks the woodbird if he will guide him to a friend and teacher. The woodbird tells Siegfried about Brünnhilde, who Wotan put to sleep on a mountain, and says that if Siegfried can pass through the flames surrounding her she shall be his bride.

Wagner has written his allegories very cleverly. The words and music accompanying these scenes can easily be interpreted as the great adventure of a young man seeking romance and a wife. But on a higher level the allegory is about a quest for spiritual enlightenment that has gone wrong. Wagner composed happy music because he knew that most people would not have the frame of reference needed to recognize the spiritual allegory. Yet it was important to catch most people's interest. In order to do that he had to have his story appear in the form of a lighthearted drama. Most of the world's great artworks work this way; having something for everyone, knowing that only a few people will appreciate the higher allegory. But it does not stop there. The simple story plants seeds so that when people are ready for higher consciousness they can recall and work with it.

What comes next is crucial to understanding *The Ring* on an esoteric level.

Wagner has used the term "unacquainted with fear" many times, to describe the person who can slay the dragon and find his (or her) higher self. Siegfried is so gifted and strong that he has never experienced fear. He has already slain the dragon, and he will find Brünnhilde (his higher self); but never having experienced fear does not mean that he has overcome it. Maybe there is something that *will* scare him. Siegfried has not been fully tested. If he had been properly initiated he would have experienced fear and overcome it. This is a major distinction. Our trials make us strong. Siegfried was not at fault. He was leading the way for humanity and had no teacher; he had to progress by trial and error. Unfortunately, his error was a big one.

The woodbird has already helped him. It is about to continue when Siegfried says:

A foolish boy,

unacquainted with fear,
dear woodbird, why, that's me!
Today in vain
I attempted to learn -
I hoped that the dragon could teach me,
now joy fills my heart,
since from Brünnhilde I'll learn it!
What way must I take to the rock? (218-19)

The woodbird leads the way, which teasingly goes in various directions before taking a definite course. The music contributes to the allegory by being joyful, playful, and happy.

The Wanderer (formerly Wotan) re-enters the picture. Through his ravens, who ancient cultures believed delivered communications between the spiritual and physical worlds, the Wanderer knows of the encounter between Siegfried and the woodbird. He hopes to prevent Siegfried from reaching Brünnhilde. He knows Siegfried is not prepared to enter the spiritual world and find his higher self, since he thinks Brünnhilde can teach him fear. Siegfried is looking to find in the spiritual world what he can only learn on the physical plane. Although the Wanderer has committed himself to not simplifying his grandson's spiritual quest, he can try to obstruct Siegfried from pursuing it before he is prepared. But how best to do this?

The Wanderer awakens Erda, the earth spirit and mother of Brünnhilde, to ask advice. Her time is past. Her wisdom is fading. She cannot help. She tells the

Wanderer that Brünnhilde can give him the answers (222), but he has put her to sleep, so that is out of the question. As the old gods are dying, so too, is Erda going into an everlasting sleep (225). The Wanderer is on his own.

Siegfried is following the woodbird, which approaches the spot where the Wanderer awaits and then flutters away "to save its life!" (229). Siegfried blithely says he'll simply follow the path himself. Soon he meets the Wanderer, who calls out to ask him where he goes. To Siegfried, the Wanderer is just an old man standing in his way, but he hopes the old man might give him more information. They have a brief dialogue, in which the Wanderer questions Siegfried about how he slew the dragon.

> Who forged your sword
> so sharp and true,
> that it slew so fierce a foe?
> Siegfried answers truthfully.
> I forged it myself
> when the smith was beaten:
> swordless else I should be.
> And the Wanderer gets to the heart of the matter:
> But who made
> the mighty fragments
> from which the sword could then be forged?

Siegfried cannot hear beyond the Wanderer's words, as he was able to with Mime. He has no idea of the Wanderer's significance, and no interest in exploring the question. With youthful confidence Siegfried replies:

Ha! How can I tell?
I only knew
that the broken sword was useless,
till I had forged it myself.

Upon which, per Wagner's stage directions, the Wanderer breaks into a happy, good-humored laugh and says, "That's certainly true!" then looks at Siegfried with approval (227).

Siegfried, though, is impatient. He accuses the Wanderer of mocking him with his questions and tells him to either help him with directions or shut up. The Wanderer tells Siegfried to be patient, a lesson he learned the hard way from Loge. He knows Siegfried is acting prematurely. Siegfried, being young and determined, tells him to mind his own business and get out of his way. He is not going to let anyone restrain him the way Mime once did.

The Wanderer says:
I see my son,
one thing you know –
to get your way as you want it.
Yet be careful,
for with eyes quite as blind
as that eye I've lost, you are gazing
on the eye that is left me for sight. (228)

The Wanderer is trying to warn Siegfried of the folly of wandering blindly into a realm for which he is not ready, but Siegfried cannot hear the Wanderer's true meaning. He interprets his words as applying to the physical plane and bursts out laughing in scorn at the "old man's" advice. The Wanderer softly bemoans the fact that youthful hero that he loves so much does not know who he is (229) but Siegfried does not hear him. He calls the Wanderer a "stubborn old fool" and tells him to get out of the way; he doesn't need help. The Wanderer warns Siegfried that the fire surrounding Brünnhilde will destroy him[20]. Siegfried has no sense of fear and advances. The Wanderer bars his way and says that the spear he holds once broke the sword that Siegfried carries, and that it will break it again if he attempts to pass. Siegfried now knows the Wanderer must be the man responsible for his father's death. He cries out a challenge:

> Then my father's foe
> faces me here?
> Glorious vengeance!
> I've found at last!
> Stretch out your spear:
> and see it break on my sword!

Siegfried draws his sword and, with a single blow, breaks the Wanderer's spear in two. The power released from the spear makes the flames around the rock burn more brightly. The Wanderer knows he is defeated. He quietly picks up the pieces of his sword and disappears,

---

[20] He is speaking the truth, but on a spiritual level.

knowing he cannot stop Siegfried. The Wanderer does not appear in *The Ring* again. This is a turning point in the story of evolution. Humanity, represented by Siegfried, is stronger than the old gods.

According to Steiner, at each point in evolution some of the leading spirits fail to progress. They remain behind in their level of consciousness and continue trying to influence people as they did previously. What was right at one time is not right at a later time, and these spirits have gone from being what we would call "good" to being "evil." Before humanity was mature enough to be free they needed the authoritative, dogmatic leadership of those gods. Now that has changed. Many old gods, who were good in their time, have failed to progress and are now trying to hold humanity back using the same authoritative, dogmatic leadership they used in the past. All of the gods in *The Ring* fall into that category with the exception of Wotan. He accepts the progression and eventually ascends to a sphere no longer directly connected with human affairs.

Siegfried turns toward the mountain, where the flames surrounding Brünnhilde have become a sea of fire sweeping down from the heights. To music that is increasingly joyful and exciting, Siegfried, pure and fearless, effortlessly traverses the flames (231). There he finds a person laying on the ground, clad in armor. Siegfried thinks this must be a man, fallen, and worries that the pressure of the helmet may be doing further injury. He carefully removes it, and is startled by the long curling hair that falls down. Siegfried still thinks he is helping a fellow man. He attempts to loosen the breastplate, but it is so heavy he cannot. Carefully, he uses his sword to cut through the metal and remove it. Brünnhilde lies before him "in soft, woman's drapery" (233). Only now does he realize this is not a man. He has never seen a woman before, and he is at once struck by wild emotion and at a loss for what to do. For the first time in his life, he feels fear (234)!

He kisses her and she awakens. She praises the day and recognizes Siegfried, then sings:

> O learn from me, joy of the world,
> how I have always loved you!
> You were my gladness,
> my cares as well!
> Your life I sheltered
> in Sieglinde's womb;
> before she had born you,
> I was your shield,
> so long have I loved, Siegfried!

For a moment Siegfried thinks he has found his mother, but Brünnhilde gently corrects him:

> O innocent child!
> Nevermore you'll look on your mother.
> But we are one,
> if you can grant me your love.
> What you would learn,
> learn it from me,
> for wisdom fills my soul,

now that I love you! (236)

From this it is clear that she i
and will be his teacher. Brünnhild
points to her horse, Grane, which
also awakened.

Things are happening fast here. According to
Steiner's esoteric teachings, fire separates the physical
world form the spiritual world. To paraphrase him, it
is not a physical fire; it is the fire of higher consciousness. People who have not adequately raised their level
of morality cannot pass through this. If they try they
will burn up. It protects people from a situation they
are unprepared for and protects the spiritual world and
its beings from them. Impurity cannot be brought into
the higher spiritual world. Siegfried, being pure, was
able to pass through the flames to find his bride and
higher self, Brünnhilde. As he awakened Brünnhilde he
also awakened her horse, Grane. In mythology horses
are a means of travel between the physical and spiritual
worlds. Brünnhilde can now travel back and forth with
Siegfried.

Brünnhilde next sees her helmet and breastplate lying nearby. While Siegfried sings of the ardor of love
and fear that have taken hold in his heart, Brünnhilde
sings sadly of the loss of her defenses. Her armor hid
her and symbolically protected her. When Siegfried
removed it she became defenseless. She is dependent
on him for protection. As Steiner has emphasized, it
is our responsibility to protect our higher self, a major

for not entering the spiritual world premature-
Fortunately for Brünnhilde Siegfried is pure and
brave, a good combination of traits for her protector.
Unfortunately for her, he does not realize he is in the
spiritual world. She wants to share her spiritual wisdom
with him (236) but he wants her to physically consum-
mate the love they have both declared. The tragic fact
that Siegfried cannot raise his awareness to the spiritual
plane is one of the most pressing issues, if not the most
pressing issue, we face today.

Siegfried can use concepts to understand and manipulate the physical environment, but he cannot apply concepts to the spiritual world. Siegfried lacks what
Steiner calls Michaelic consciousness; the ability to understand the spiritual world with the same exactness we
have in our physical environment. Using the language
of percepts and concepts, in *A Philosophy of Freedom*
Steiner explains that our percepts are for the physical
plane; concepts for the spiritual plane; and all thinking
is a spiritual activity.[21] The problem is that we don't recognize it as a spiritual activity. We perceive thinking as a
mechanical process that takes place within our physical
brains. The process of transitioning from concepts on
the physical plane to concepts on the spiritual plane is

---

[21] A percept is an impression you receive through your physical
senses. A concept is an idea. In my vernacular, a percept is active
in the left brain and a concept is active in the right brain. In the
fourth cultural epoch a person's concepts were limited relative to
their perceptions, thus limiting our freedom of thinking. What
Steiner brilliantly noted is how a concept can be treated as a percept to foster higher consciousness.

what we have to develop during the present, fifth, cultural epoch. Steiner explained how to do this in several of his books and lecture series, especially *Knowledge of Higher Worlds*. The inability to carry concepts into the spiritual world has been an ongoing problem, especially since the Renaissance. Brilliant thinkers, including Christopher Columbus, Francis Bacon, and Sir Isaac Newton, failed to recognize the difference and, as a result, they felt the spiritual world was just an extension of the physical realm and subject to the laws of physics. It is time to rise above this.

Steiner has said that we will only understand the spiritual world when we get there, to the extent that we have learned to understand it while on Earth. We "fell" to earth to learn in a more concrete environment what we could not learn in the ethereal realm. The metaphor could be used about us seeing the trees, and higher spiritual beings seeing the forest: we need each other to arrive at truth. The higher spirits can clarify and enhance what we know, but they can't teach us the ABC's.

Siegfried had no *frame of reference* for what he encountered. Although he is descended from a god and is clearly a hero (initiate) his life on Earth included no spiritual training or insight. Is it any wonder that in his encounters with the Guardian of the Threshold, the woodcock, and the Wanderer, Siegfried continued to behave according to the rules and behaviors of Earth? Brünnhilde could now be his spiritual guide but since he looks upon her from the physical plane, he sees her as his physical bride, not as his higher self.

Wagner's music is upbeat in these scenes, and this is usually taken as a boy-meets-girl, boy-gets-girl story. On a higher plane it is much more serious. Siegfried tells Brünnhilde that the flames that guarded her rock now burn fiercely in his heart, and that only she can douse them. Brünnhilde is shocked and offended: he wants her body, not her wisdom! She pushes him away and flees to the other side of the stage, terrified and grieved at her vulnerable state.

> No god dared to come near!
> The heroes bowed
> and knelt to the maiden:
> holy came she from Valhalla.
> Sorrow! Sorrow!
> Woe for my shame,
> how keen my disgrace!
> And he who wakes me
> deals me the wound!
> He has broken breastplate and helm:
> Brünnhilde I am no more! (239)

Siegfried says that she is still Brünnhilde, and thinks she must still be sleeping. He calls out, "Awaken, you are my bride!"

Brünnhilde pleads with him:

> Leave, ah, leave,
> leave me in peace!
> Do not come near me
> with passionate frenzy;

do not pursue me
with masterful might,
or else you'll destroy all our love! (240)

She warns him that his actions will destroy their love and her (241). He persists, begging her to love him and quench the fire that burns in him. He ardently embraces her, and at last she succumbs.

Godly composure
change into wildness;
virginal light,
flare into frenzy;
heavenly wisdom,
fly to the winds …
… Siegfried! Siegfried!
Can you not see?
When my eyes blaze on you,
then are you not blind? …
Tell me then, Siegfried,
do you not fear
this wild, passionate maid? (242)

But as this takes place, Siegfried finds that the fear he first felt with her is gone.

I find again
my boldness of heart;
and what fear is, ah!
I have failed to learn;
what fear is, not even
you can teach!

My fear, I find,
has faded and gone like a dream! (243)

The one common thread in pre-fifth cultural epoch initiations was that the initiates entered them in a dream-like state, not in full consciousness. They would undergo an experience, and then recollect their experiences in the same way they might remember a dream.[22]

Brünnhilde loves Siegfried completely and finally yields to his wishes, though realizing they will die in their laughter (243-44). The final curtain comes down on the opera *Siegfried*.

It would be naïve think this is the end of a beautiful boy meets girl story, but it would also be naïve to think nothing good will come from it. Brünnhilde has made it clear that she may be dying as far as the old gods are concerned, but she is now living in the potentially clear light of Siegfried. Whether one takes their love affair as a sexual encounter or a spiritual union, she has firmly rejected the old gods. By uniting with Siegfried they can accomplish a great deal. But the problem remains: Siegfried still does not realize he is in the spiritual

---

[22] Another difference is that in times previous, initiations were carried out by a hierophant, or spiritual leader, in secrecy. Candidates were highly prepared, especially in terms of morality and courage. Today that has changed. People may have a guide but he or she will be little more than a guide. We have to take responsibility for ourselves. Instead of preparations taking place in secrecy they occur in our everyday lives as we interact with others. An excellent book on this subject is Harry Salmon's *Initiation in the Social World*.

world. Steiner has said our principle task in the fifth cultural epoch is to understand the spiritual world. Before the fifth cultural epoch people did not have the ability to understand the spiritual world. Religion's task was to keep the idea of the spiritual world alive, not to explain it. In spite of all their abuses the major world religions succeeded at that. They did so by appealing to the senses, not the intellect. Today we can and should learn to understand the spiritual world.

CHAPTER 8

FEAR

The story of *The Ring* is the history of the evolution of consciousness. In it Wagner makes it clear that fearlessness is a prerequisite to the development of higher consciousness. The subject of fear is so prominent in *The Ring* that it deserves further attention.

In *The Valkyrie* Brünnhilde pleads with Wotan:

… let only one
who is fearless and free
none but a hero
find me here! (149)
In Siegfried Wotan tells Mime:
'One who has never
learnt to fear -
he makes [the sword] new.'
Your wily head -
guard it with care!
I leave it forfeit to him
who has never learnt to fear. (176)

The woodbird tells Siegfried:

Who wakens the maid,
Brünnhilde the bride,
no coward can be:
one unacquainted with fear! (218)

This reinforces what we have already learned. Siegfried then points out that he is the fearless one (219).

> A foolish boy,
> unacquainted with fear,
> dear woodbird, why, that's me!

The Wanderer tells Erda, who is both the Earth Spirit and Brünnhilde's mother:

> Free from hate,
> joyful and loving,
> [Siegfried] is not harmed
> by Alberich's curse,
> for he knows naught of fear. (234)

There are many ways to examine the issue of fear. The approach I will focus on has to do with advances in the evolution of consciousness during the third, fourth, and fifth 2,160-year cycles, and how Siegfried is limited by these in regards to his fearlessness.

Dictionaries define fear as anxiety or apprehension regarding a possible danger. The key words here are *po-* which may or may not happen. The energy associated with fear is a two-edged sword. On a lower level that energy can easily incapacitate a person. It is a lower state of consciousness. On a higher level, the same energy instigates courage. On a lower level panic or despondency occurs. On a higher level a person can adapt all their resources to problem solving.

Fear belongs to the third 2,160-year evolutionary cycle, the age of the sentient soul. During this period the physical senses were introduced to humanity. Along with the ability to touch, smell, hear, see, etc., came certain emotional responses, some of which were automatic (an infant being afraid of falling), while some were conditioned (after burning your hand you learn to automatically keep your hand away from fire). This was good: after all if we had to relearn these responses every time, life would be a whole lot more difficult.

In the fourth cultural epoch the ability to think rationally and intellectually was developed. Then, at least theoretically, we could overrule automatic reactions which were not serving our purposes. But there were two problems associated with this. First, our automatic responses were so firmly entrenched that we often did not have the ability to overrule them, even if we knew it was to our advantage. Second, unsavory characters who did not want people to be free (a free person cannot be controlled or exploited) learned to manipulate our automatic responses. This would later become the standard for training animals: punish or reward them repeatedly for certain types of behavior and soon they will anticipate what is wanted from them and respond automatically without the punishment or reward. During the third and fourth 2,160-year cycles people were operating on an animalistic level and this worked very effectively. Fear was the strongest of emotions and the one most easily utilized for the purpose of manipulation. During the fourth epoch the potential to overcome our automatic responses became a reality, but people are slow to respond to change and many remained stuck in the same conditions which existed in the previous epoch.

In *The Valkyrie*, Siegmund and Sieglinde are locked into the third epoch conditions. It was, after all, still the third cycle. They are ahead of their time in that they seek freedom and love, but they die trying. In *Siegfried*, Siegfried starts out in third epoch consciousness but his curious mind keeps him asking questions about higher consciousness. These questions have to do with concepts or ideas. He develops the ability to think analytically and finds answers to many of his questions; however, his ideas, and those of the fourth epoch in general, are limited to the physical realm. He is not able to perform sense-free thinking, or to put it differently, to form concepts about the spiritual world. This creates a big problem when he enters the spiritual world. His only frame of reference is the physical world, and he thinks he is still in that world when he is not. Siegfried is briefly acquainted with fear upon seeing Brünnhilde, but what might have become his foundation for wisdom is quickly lost in passion. Thinking Brünnhilde is a physical person, Siegfried selfishly focuses his thoughts on me, me, me. Her pleas for him to rise up to her level are totally overruled, and Siegfried remains in the spiritual world without the ability to think thoughts based on something other than physical perception. He continues acting on a lower level of consciousness, and this leaves him unequipped to recognize his enemies.

When Wagner repeatedly states that only a person who is not subject to fear can find Brünnhilde (the hero's higher self) it can be inferred that only a man more advanced in cosmic consciousness will reach that spiritual plane. Siegfried demonstrates the fourth epoch's ability to use the intellect and does find Brünnhilde; but he does not have the fifth epoch's ability to apply his intellect to spiritual knowledge. He gets in through the back door, so to speak, entering with a fearlessness that has never known fear. Siegfried's entry into the spiritual world without proper preparation results in disaster, as it does in all human experience.

Siegfried looked to Brünnhilde to teach him fear, but fear is something that must be mastered on the earthly plane. Fear brings us into the world of parts-and-pieces, which is a lower state of consciousness than the oneness of the spiritual world. Fear can cause us to compartmentalize our being. Fear can cause a person to focus on narrow issues so intently that he or she is not capable of functioning on a higher plane. The "fall" was a fall into parts-and-pieces that allowed humanity to develop individual consciousness. Now our task is to be able to operate on the spiritual plane with individual consciousness intact. To re-forge the sword – or find and awaken one's higher self – one must rise above the silos of left brain thinking and see or understand the whole. Overcoming fear and its consequences requires higher consciousness.

Of all the emotions associated with physical perceptions, fear is the most pronounced. Sometimes fear is instinctive, such as what an infant experiences at the prospect of falling; sometimes it is a conditioned response that develops from painful experience; and sometimes it is an artificially-induced emotion set up by someone we trust (i.e. a political or religious leader, a spokesperson, etc.) Regardless of the cause or reason fear is the most powerful of emotions to a person whose level of consciousness is most strongly tied into that of the physical senses. When Wagner makes the point that only a person who is not dominated by fear can make the sword anew, have control over those (like Mime) who wish to dominate them, find his (or her) higher self (Brünnhilde), and awaken that higher self, he is saying that a person must raise their consciousness in order to find freedom.

In the fifth epoch, thinking was freed from the physical world after Michael resumed leadership in 1879. People were free to use thinking to understand the spiritual world. The time has come when we can understand the spiritual world; yet, in the fifth epoch many people are still locked into third epoch conditions and manipulated on the animalistic level through fear. Steiner taught that our task in this generation is to recognize evil so that we can transform it. This requires that we understand what is happening on the physical and spiritual plane. To paraphrase Wagner, in order to re-forge their sword, live free from domination, and find and awaken his or her higher self a person must develop consciousness free of fear; or higher than the sense-based form that held sway in the third cultural epoch.

Chapter 9:

The Manipulation of Siegfried

The higher spirits cannot do evil, but as Rudolf Steiner points out they can direct evil into channels in which it will eventually do less harm. When Lucifer fell and took "us" with him, the fall was directed in such a way that individuality would be established. In the spiritual world boundaries and edges are not well defined: it is difficult, sometimes impossible, to know where one begins and ends. Think of a drop of oil in the ocean. Where does it begin and end? When Lucifer "fell" he went through the process described earlier; part of him refining and part condensing. The lower part took us with him. He was able to do this because humanity had not established boundaries (individuality) so we were, as one might say, easy pickings. Our energy was available for whoever was strong and determined enough to take it, and Lucifer took it. This "energy" was made up of the lower, condensed portions of the various hierarchies, so they were actually losing parts of themselves. According to Steiner the higher spirits realized what was happening but could not stop it. But they did make sure it would happen in a way that would eventually result in good. Such principles are evident in Wagner's portrayal of activities

in Valhalla during *Twilight of the Gods*, and the final
words attributed to Wotan.

In Scene 3 of *Twilight of the Gods* Waltraute – a
Valkyrie and Brünnhilde's spiritual sister – visits
Brünnhilde. At first Brünnhilde hopes her sister has
come to deliver Wotan's pardon. Waltraute tells her
that Wotan is not the bold and fear-inducing god he
once was, but is "enthroned in silence, stern and sad."
She describes a scene that shows Wotan is aware that
the ring's drama is unfolding on Earth, yet he takes no
warrior-like actions to stop them. Instead, he has the
sacred branches of the World Ash-tree broken up and
"pile[d] in a heap all around the glorious hall," as if to
burn it. Then he calls "the holy clan" to sit with him,
and stations his heroes in ranks around the hall, where
they "look on in silence."

> He has sent his ravens
> forth on their journeys;
> when they return
> and bring the news he awaits,
> then for the last time
> a smile of joy
> will shine on the face of the god. (274)

Waltraute describes how she wept on Wotan's
breast, and how his "glance grew more mild" as he remembered Brünnhilde. Waltraute says Wotan then

> sighed in grief,
> closed his eye,

and deep in dreaming,
whispered these words:
'If once the Rhine's fair daughters
win back their ring from Brünnhilde again,
then the curse will pass;
she will save both god and the world!' (274-75)

Those are Wotan's final words in *The Ring Cycle*, and they inspire Waltraute to visit Brünnhilde and plead with her to return *the ring* to the Rhinemaidens (275). Wotan has not directly interfered, but his words will influence events away from evil. Though Brünnhilde calls Waltraute's request "madness" in this scene, by the end of the opera she will gaze at *the ring* and sing:

You sisters
who are wise and graceful,
you Rhinemaids who dwell in the waters,
I shall obey your advice.
What you desire
I'll give to you … (327)

Brünnhilde's changed attitude toward *the ring*'s destiny comes about as a consequence of Siegfried's manipulation by evil forces.

If a person's individuality is not established, or if they are ignorant, they can be relatively easily manipulated. Siegfried's individuality was well established, but his ignorance remained immense.

Spiritual beings (for example those beings that we perceive as stars) guide, or impel, human beings. Fear not: this does not even come close to meaning that we do not have free will. Humans are endowed with free will, though people who are limited to lower consciousness are often slaves to their emotions and feelings, and as a result are easily manipulated by those who take advantage of their lower state of consciousness. As we develop our higher consciousness we gradually become freer. Spiritual beings do not compel people operating from higher consciousness to do anything; however, the closer we follow the path which they are impelling us to take the more freedom, love, and creative capacity we develop. How we make use of their guidance is up to us. In the epilogue I will go into more detail about how forces counter to evolution are using spiritual principles in ways counter to the ideals of freedom: those forces want their idea of god to control the masses so as to deprive humanity of freedom. In the ongoing battle over human freedom, the higher spirits cannot use force or deceit, but the lower spirits have no holds barred. In The *Twilight of the Gods* Wagner gives several examples of how the lower forces operate.

The driving force of evil in *Twilight of the Gods* is Alberich/Ahriman. The opposite of not having established one's identity or ego is becoming so individualized that one is completely isolated. In that case one does not realize there is a spiritual world or, if it is recognized, it is rejected. This is the case with Alberich. He has formed a ring around himself which isolates him from the rest of creation. He knows it exists but he wants the "world" to be within his "ring," with himself in control as the god. To achieve this he will use and manipulate others in any way he can.

In *The Valkyrie*, we are told that

[Alberich] has forced a woman;
his gold bought her embrace
and she will bear
Alberich's son:
the seed of spite
stirs in her womb;
this wonder befell
the loveless Niblung ... (111)

It must be remembered that Alberich is not a physical being. Mythology is full of examples of spiritual beings mating with physical beings. The esoteric interpretation is that in the days before the intellectual soul people were not capable of leading themselves or taking spiritual instruction in a fully conscious state. Spiritual beings led them by what we would call possession. Alberich wants an emissary through whom he can bring *the ring* back under his control. Whether Alberich's mother was forced against her will or sold herself for money is not clear. In any case there is no warmth in the conception, the perfect set up for Alberich/Ahriman whose nature is coldness.

In *Twilight of the Gods* we meet Alberich's son, Hagen, who describes himself as:

Old in youth, gaunt and pale,
hating the happy (282)
Alberich comes to Hagen at night and tells him:
Cherish that hatred!
Then your unhappy
joyless father
you will love as you should!
Now be cunning,
strong and bold!
Those whom with weapons
of darkness we fight,
soon they shall be destroyed by our hate. (282)
I and you!
The world shall be ours,
if I can trust
my scheming son,
if truly you share my hate. (283)

Wagner's stage directions indicate that Hagen is asleep when Alberich arrives. Alberich speaks to him, and Hagen replies, "softly, without moving, so that he appears to be sleeping on although his eyes are open" (282). Hagen remains in a trance as the Alberich delivers his commands: the loveless Niblung does not approach even his own son in full consciousness.

Alberich urges Hagen to swear he will avenge his father and win *the ring* for him, and at that point dawn begins to break. Every time dawn is presented, night ending, or the sun shining it is symbolic of clear consciousness; not the foggy consciousness which existed earlier. I'd like to turn now, to the Prelude to *Twilight of the Gods*, which starts with dawn breaking over the flame-protected rock upon which Siegfried discovered Brünnhilde.

Siegfried and Brünnhilde have physically united. They are married, but he is now leaving her behind, for deeds of glory (252) and more adventures (261). In esoteric language "adventures" mean initiation tests. In other words, Siegfried has not completed his initiation on Earth so he must return and try to do it right. Unfortunately, he still does not recognize that there is a difference between the physical and spiritual worlds.

Brünnhilde has given him all her wisdom and strength, leaving her vulnerable but rich in love (253). She fears, and rightfully so, that Siegfried will abandon her now that she has nothing left to give (253). Siegfried admits that in spite of her lessons he is still ignorant, but says that what he has truly learnt is that he loves her. He pledges his love for her, and they agree that when they are separated they will still be one (255). He gives her *the ring* as a token of his love, and she gives him her horse, Grane, which has lost its enchanted power to fly through lightning and thunder but will bear Siegfried without fear on the earthly plane (254).

Siegfried, the grandson of Wotan, has the means to rule the world but is unaware of its significance. Hagen, the son of Alberich, has been schooled in its significance and is determined to acquire that means any way he can. Hagen's half brother is King Gunther: they share the same mother. Gunther's half-sister is

Gutrune: they share the same father. King Gunther, Hagen and Gutrune live together in a great Hall on the Rhine, for which Siegfried is bound.

Gunther is not a bad man. Steiner says he and his sister represent average people. However, Gunther does not have a strong sense of identity: he looks to Hagen for guidance.

In the opening scene of Act 1, Hagen, cunningly exhibits the influence of Alberich/Ahriman. He tells Gunther he needs a wife and that, being king, he deserves a person who can enhance his status. Hagen then describes Brünnhilde: "the noblest woman in the world" who will be bride to the hero who braves the fire encircling her (258). Gunther asks whether his own strength is great enough to make him that hero, and Hagen says, frankly, that it is not; but he then describes Siegfried and his feat of killing the dragon that hoarded the famous gold. Hagen suggests his plan:

"What if Siegfried
would win the bride –
might he not give her to you? (260)

Gunther asks how such a thing could possibly come about, and Hagen hatches his plan. He explains that he can give Siegfried a magic drink that will make him forget Brünnhilde and long to marry Gutrune. Once Siegfried falls for Gutrune, it will be easy for Gunther to have him act on his behalf. The plan is set: Gutrune will give Siegfried the magical drink which will make him forget the past (261). In esoteric literature this magical drink is sometimes called the draught of forgetfulness, and Steiner discusses it in various lectures. When a person incarnates at birth, or when one awakens from sleep, their just-completed experience in the spiritual world is forgotten. The intellect, which is in the domain of Ahriman, is the veil which destroys our memories of it.

Siegfried comes rowing down the River Rhine with Brünnhilde's horse on board. Like horses, boats are often used in mythology to signify transportation between worlds. The significance of the River Rhine is that according to German mythology, as the gods were disappearing from Earth the last place they dwelt was in the clouds which formed over the Alps. The water which condensed on the mountaintops still contained a vestige of their being. The droplets converged, forming the River Rhine. That is where the Rhinemaidens live, and it is where Siegfried arrives on Earth from the spiritual world.

Hagen welcomes Siegfried as he arrives and volunteers to care for the horse. Gunther welcomes Siegfried, and they pledge their fealty to one another. Gunther says Siegfried may share in his birthright, and command his men and him. In return Siegfried says all he has, his body and his sword, now belong to Gunther. Hagen joins them, and questions Siegfried about the Niblung's gold. Siegfried tells him that he left it in the cave, since it was valueless to him. Hagen asks whether he took anything from the cave, and Siegfried points to the tarnhelm which hangs from his belt. He tells Hagen that he doesn't know its purpose, and Hagen enlightens him as to its magical powers. Then Hagen asks Siegfried whether he took anything else from the cave, and Siegfried says he took a ring, which he has left, "Kept safe on a fair woman's hand" (265).

Gutrune enters the hall and gives Siegfried the magic drink. As he drinks, Gutrune looks down in shame and confusion (265). She is ashamed of her deceit, but she carries through her part in the plan. The potion works instantly, and Siegfried expresses his ardent admiration for Gutrune. He then asks Gunther whether he has a wife. Gunther describes the noble maid he would hope to marry, but for the fact that he fears the flames surrounding her. As Gunther describes Brünnhilde he uses phrases that the woodcock used when describing her to Siegfried. At first, Siegfried expresses some memory of the words, but their significance escapes him. But when Gunther states Brünnhilde's name, it is clear that Siegfried has no recollection of her.

Siegfried is soon volunteering to brave the flames on Gunther's behalf. He plans to use the tarnhelm to disguise himself as Gunther, reasoning that when he arrives on the rock in that form, Brünnhilde will believe that Gunther himself is the fearless hero worthy of her hand. Siegfried and Gunther then undergo a ritual to become blood brothers. They swear to the death to be loyal to each other. Hagen holds the wine-filled horn into which they let their blood drop, and when they have drunk from it Hagen strikes the horn in two with his own sword. Siegfried asks Hagen why he did not take part in the oath, and Hagen replies that his blood is cold (a characteristic of Ahriman as well as Alberich), and if he took part in their fiery vows he would spoil it for them (268). The blood oath Gunther and Siegfried takes is a Luciferic affair, hot and "fiery" (269). If the Ahrimanic element had been included it would have cooled the pact. Steiner often tells about Lucifer and Ahriman working together when it suits their selfish needs. This is an example.

Siegfried and Gunther sail away to get Brünnhilde. Hagen says to himself:

> … With her, he brings me *the ring*!
> you sons of freedom,
> joyful companions,
> merrily sail on your way!
> Though you despise me,
> you'll serve me soon,
> the Niblung's son. (270)

A lot has happened in the beginning of The *Twilight of the Gods*. Before continuing let's take a closer look at the ramifications of the situation Wagner presents. First of all we have been told Hagen is the representative of evil. Gunther does not seem like a bad person, but he is a weak character who envies his half-brother Hagen and looks to him for wisdom. By appealing to his pride (a Luciferic quality) with a forecast of "fame and wonderful treasures," Hagen persuades Gunther to marry Brünnhilde. To arrange that, Hagen – through

Gunther and Gutrune – will manipulate Siegfried into betraying Brünnhilde. For Hagen's plan to work, Siegfried must be given the draught of forgetfulness and take Gutrune for a wife. This illustrates an important point. The lower spirits, like Hagen, cannot enter the relatively higher realms of the spiritual world, let alone the very high realms. To exert their influence in those realms they need humans to work for them. If people were to come across as evil spirits or humans recruiting other people to do their dirty work, they would have limited success at best. In ancient times when fear and force held sway subtlety may not have been a common trait among manipulators, but in this age where people can reason, the forces of evil have to be more discrete. By using discretion and secrecy they can fool or manipulate good but ignorant, weak, or desperate people into doing their bidding. Hagen is out to get Siegfried to yield his higher power to him. There are a lot of people who thrive on doing just that. The prerequisite for their success is to appear friendly and good, or to work through people who appear that way. That is the situation Wagner illustrates here.

Although he does not remember it, Siegfried has already made it through the flames and won his spiritual bride, his higher self, Brünnhilde. In the process he has disarmed her and she is powerless, but she has *the ring* which has the power. Siegfried is about to give Brünnhilde to Gunther, who will, in turn, give it to Hagen, who will then give it, or at least the use of it, to Alberich, who will then have control of the world. This may sound like the stuff pulp fiction thrives on but it is a serious allegory for the ongoing struggle between good and evil in our everyday lives. In the case of Siegfried he is good and he is highly motivated to serve what he sees as the higher good, but he is ignorant of the battle being played out between proponents of higher and lower consciousness. Out of love for who he thinks are his new friends he falls into their trap and volunteers to do everything his enemies want, without even being asked. Steiner has said our most important task today is to understand the spiritual world, a lesson Siegfried has not learned.

Siegfried, impersonating Gunther, reaches Brünnhilde, and claims her as "his" bride. She says *the ring* will defend her, but he takes *the ring* from her finger and places it on his own. Brünnhilde thinks that Gunther now wears *the ring*. She falls unconscious. Siegfried-as-Gunther sends her into a cave and enters it behind her. The next morning, Siegfried uses the tarnhelm to transport himself back to the Hall on the Rhine, while Gunther sails toward the Hall with Brünnhilde aboard. The opera is not half over but Siegfried, acting in good faith, has been manipulated into turning his higher powers over to the forces of evil.

Hagen manipulates characters and events in subtle ways, and he and Gunther plan to murder Siegfried while on a hunt. During the hunt, Siegfried separates from the group and encounters the Rhinemaidens as he rests near the river. They ask Siegfried for *the ring* and him about *the ring*'s history and the death curse that Alberich laid upon it. Unfortunately, Siegfried takes this as a challenge and threat. He had decided to give them *the ring*, but his pride makes him change his mind.

> The world's wealth
> I could win me by this ring:
> for a glance of love
> I would exchange it;
> if you had smiled *the ring* would be yours.
> But you threatened my limbs and my life:
> now though *the ring*
> had no worth at all,
> you'd still not get it from me. (311)

To which the Rhinemaidens say:

> Come, sisters!
> Flee from this madman!
> He thinks he is wise,
> he thinks he is strong,
> but he's stupid and blind as a child! (312)

They marvel at Siegfried's folly. He had in his grasp the highest gift of all, in the form of Brünnhilde, and threw it away; but now he holds onto *the ring* that will bring his death.

> You die today;
> and your ring returns to Brünnhilde;
> by her, our prayer will be heard:
> To her! To her! To her! (312)

The hunting party rejoins Siegfried. Hagen says

I've heard it rumored, Siegfried
that when the birds are singing
you know what they say:
but can that be true?

Siegfried replies:

For a long while I've paid
no heed to their song. (315)
… Since women have sung their songs to me,
I've cared for the birdsong no more.

Hagen draws Siegfried into a conversation about
the past, and gives Siegfried a drink with an herb that
will lift the veil of forgetfulness. Siegfried drinks, and
recalls that he is Brünnhilde's husband. He says so much
in his tale of the past. Two ravens appear, and dusk
begins to fall. Hagen thrusts his spear into Siegfried's
back. With his dying breaths, Siegfried sings:

Brünnhilde!
Holiest bride!
Now wake! Wake from your slumber!
Who has forced you
back to your sleep?
Who bound you in slumber again?
Your bridegroom came,
to kiss you awake;
he frees you, again,
breaking your fetters. (320)

As he is dying, Siegfried recognizes Brünnhilde as his higher spiritual self, his holiest bride.

The scene shifts back to the Hall, where it is night. The hunting party returns, bearing Siegfried's body and the tale that he was killed by a wild boar. Gutrune does not believe them and cries out that Siegfried was murdered. Gunther immediately tells her it was Hagen's spear. Hagen and Gunther begin to fight over *the ring*. Siegfried's hand raises itself threateningly, which freezes everyone in fear. Brünnhilde enters. Gutrune blames her for the evil that's befallen them. Brünnhilde says:

> Poor creature, peace!
> For you and he were not wed;
> his mistress,
> but never his wife! (325)

Gutrune admits that Brünnhilde is right, and curses Hagen for having given them such evil advice. She sees that Brünnhilde was, indeed, Siegfried's true love.

Brünnhilde instructs the vassals to lay a funeral pyre for the fallen hero. As they build it, Brünnhilde sings Siegfried's praises. She then addresses her words to the heavens:

> … Wotan, hear,
> you mighty god!
> By his most valiant deed
> he fulfilled your desire,
> but he was forced

to share in your curse …
He, truest of all men,
betrayed me,
that I in grief might grow wise!
Now I know what must be.
All things, all things,
all I know now;
all to me is revealed!
Call back your ravens
hovering round me;
they'll bring to you those tidings
you have both feared and desired.
Rest now, rest now, O god! (326)

Brünnhilde takes *the ring* from Siegfried's finger and declares:

This fire, burning my frame,
cleanses the curse from *the ring*!

Brünnhilde lights the funeral pyre. She sees Grane, led in by servants. She removes his bridle, indicating he is a creature of free will, and speaks to him. She and Grane willingly leap to the funeral pyre, where they are consumed along with Siegfried's body. The water from the Rhine overflows its banks and floods over the fire. Hagen rushes forward. He and *the ring* are taken under the water by the Rhinemaidens. Valhalla appears in the sky, bright flames upon it. It is consumed by flame, and then the curtain falls.

This is not a happy ending. Although the forces of evil fail to seize full-power, by returning *the ring* to the River Rhine Wagner indicates that a new level of human consciousness has failed to make its debut. Evolution is back where it was at the beginning of *The Ring Cycle*. Apparently Wagner believed, when he wrote these four operas, that the best we could hope for was a return to the state humanity was in before the fall. Certainly he felt that was the highest level that could be attained at that time, which was the mid 1800s.

Wagner composed only one more opera after the completion of *The Ring*. That opera was *Parsifal*. His previous operas are pagan in nature. *Parsifal* is Christian-based. It was not until the end of his life that Wagner became a Christian, and even then, he was not a traditional Christian. His disdain for authority and dogma was too strong to submit himself to an authoritative, dogmatic, religious leader or movement. He became an esoteric Christian – a Christian who would seek answers within his own soul rather than becoming a member of a church that would look to others for answers or interpret spiritual texts from a literal (left-bran) perspective. In his opera *Parsifal*, Wagner takes *The Ring* to the next level. In that standalone opera, Wagner shows the leading initiate of the time transforming the powers of darkness through esoteric Christianity. This Christianity is basically the same form of Christianity that Rudolf Steiner taught.

Before looking at *Parsifal*, however, we will return to the subject of manipulation, this time as it has been used throughout history, leading to the present day. This was the purpose of Wagner's operas: to show the dangers of manipulation and the importance of freedom. If he had written a dissertation on the subject and had it published it would have been read by a few and forgotten. Few, if any, lives would have been changed. But by creating a great work of art, Wagner gave his message a form that has remained alive for a century and a half and is going on stronger than ever. Every year in North America some opera company produces *The Ring*. In Europe it is even more popular. Often these productions are altered almost beyond recognition, but that is what opera companies do to keep audiences coming back. This used to upset me greatly, but I now accept it as a fact of life. The important thing is that these operas are being kept alive. Those interested in understanding the opera's higher meanings have much more to work with than they would if the operas were produced as Wagner insisted upon. *The Ring* and *Parsifal* are too esoteric to be interpreted without reference to the work of esoteric scholars. Fortunately, Rudolf Steiner provided information that allows interested students to penetrate the veil that surrounds these operas.

CHAPTER 10
THE TRANSFORMATION OF EVIL

The character Parsifal is based on an actual historical personality. That person was Mani, the early Christian-era founder of the Manicheans. Without going into the details of Manichean beliefs, suffice it to say they believed in the transformation of evil, not the destruction of it. It is easy to see that Wagner was an adherent to this belief, at least in his later years. Siegfried failed to even to try transforming the powers of evil, but Parsifal spontaneously does. There was a major change in Wagner in his later years, and *Parsifal* reflects this.

Most artists say more in their works than they are aware of, and Wagner certainly followed suit. He was a passionate man who experienced life's ups and downs. Siegmund was determined to experience freedom and love independent of the gods, and was killed in the process. Siegfried was as strong and confident but failed to recognize his spiritual enemies, and was murdered by them. Parsifal spends a lifetime searching for higher consciousness (although he would not have called it that at the time) and he finally finds it. It is inconceivable that these characters were not based on Wagner's own experiences.

Wagner was also experienced in all the ups and downs of love. His feelings for separation, temptation, and longing are all expressed in his operas. The passion expressed in Wotan's farewell to Brünnhilde, both in the libretto and the music, goes far beyond what a neophyte could produce. Parsifal experiences temptations from Kundry that could not be expressed by a person who had not been subjected to similar tests. Wagner's characters give voice to his experience.

It has been said that Wagner created the opera *Parsifal* because audiences of *The Ring* wanted a happy ending. A closer inspection of his operas, however, shows that Wagner's spiritual outlook had changed. *The Ring* is a pagan work which allegorically shows the evolution of consciousness as far as Wagner could take it at the time, but it did not do justice to his new wisdom. *Parsifal* is a Christian work but not in the traditional sense of exoteric Christianity, in which people are told, directly or indirectly, what to believe. Wagner's form of Christianity was esoteric Christianity, which comes from within one's soul as the result of individual effort. Comparing the ideology in *The Ring* to the ideology in *Parsifal* makes it clear that Wagner's spiritual outlook had changed. Nevertheless, that does not make *The Ring* superfluous. *The Ring* shows the evolution of consciousness from the fall until the dawning of the present age. *The Ring* and *Parsifal* present one, continuous story.

Parsifal takes place in a medieval setting but the allegorical content is consistent with that of *The Ring*.

Wagner's description of the first scene in *Parsifal* tells us that the castle of the Grail's guardians is set in a country that is similar to the northern mountains of Gothic Spain. In the same paragraph he says Klingsor's castle is on the southern slope of the same mountains and faces Moorish Spain (GOL, 105[23]). Since the Grail guardians are "the good guys" and Klingsor is the "bad guy," Wagner seems to be making a statement that the Moors are bad and the northerners, Christians, are good. Wagner was adamantly against spiritual and religious rigidity, and the Islamic faith would be in the rigid category for him – but there is more to it than that. Rather than taking potshots at religions he disapproved of, he is saying that it is time to take a new direction, upwards and onwards. Wagner did not like any religion that was dogmatic, authoritarian, or otherwise exoteric in nature, be it Christianity, Judaism, Islam, etc. As Parsifal's story will show, Wagner was advocating a mode of belief that involved understanding and finding truth within; for him, that truth was embedded in esoteric Christianity. In his theology, Christ is not the trivial character many religions make him out to be, but a spirit with a very high level of consciousness with which we freely unite as we attain higher levels of consciousness.

In the same paragraph that he describes the castle, Wagner describes the clothing of the guardians of the

---

[23] For complete bibliographic information see the copyright page of this book.

Grail. It is similar to that of the Knights Templar, except that the Templar's red cross is replaced by a dove flying upwards. The Knights Templar was a military order of monks known for fighting during the Crusades. The cross on their clothing symbolized the crucifixion of Christ, and its color symbolized blood. Since they were a fighting order the blood may have been doubly appropriate. The dove indicates a level of higher consciousness, such as that of the Holy Ghost or Holy Spirit, for which a dove is the traditional symbol. Wagner's fight is no longer one of armed combat with the intent of destroying the enemy. In *Parsifal*, his message is of achieving higher consciousness from within and transforming evil, rather than destroying it.

In the opening scene we learn that the Knights are searching for "balsams and soothing potions" to heal their injured leader, Amfortas. Presumably, like the Templars these Knights of the Grail would have spent three centuries in Arab lands, and would be very familiar with Arab culture, which was much more advanced in many ways than that of Europeans. The Knights obviously respect the Arab's healing arts, and in this story Sir Gawain and the sorceress Kundry both look to Arabia for "balsams and soothing potions" to cure their leader's injuries (GOL 106-107, 109). It clearly states that the Arabs had nothing available to cure Amfortas, but the fact that they were looking elsewhere indicates the Europeans didn't have anything either.

Parsifal's father had been killed in battle before Parsifal's birth. His mother is determined to protect

Parsifal from such a fate and has raised him in the woods, away from anything that might encourage him to follow in his father's footsteps; very similar to Siegfried's upbringing. If we read into this a little bit it seems we are being told that Parsifal was raised in a manner that merits a deeper discussion.

During the third cultural epoch atavistic clairvoyance was fading. The kings and other leaders had been highly clairvoyant, but they too were losing their clairvoyance. The physical senses had replaced and were obliterating that clairvoyance. Without the ability to lead from a clairvoyant perspective, leaders were beginning to be perceived by the people as just ordinary human beings. In attempts to stave off this shift in belief, many royal families raised the child who was next in line in a way that kept them isolated from common daily realities; in a way that would stifle what we now refer to as the left brain functions.[24] This child would not be exposed to any of the influences that take people into the mundane world. They would have difficulty functioning in the "real" world but, if all went according to plan, they would never see it. Nothing blocks right brain development more than left brain, intellectual thinking. This would allow the right brain to flourish, at least relatively speaking. With their higher-level, atavistic clairvoyance somewhat preserved, these royal personages could rule from a higher consciousness, although they would be inept at surviving on the streets.

---

[24] A good book that hints at this, without going into esoteric realms, is *Akhenaten: Egypt's False Prophet* by Nicholas Reeves (Thames and Hudson, London, 2005).

However, times were changing and even these rulers continued to lose their clairvoyance. People were no longer looking up to them as gods.

Buddha was raised this way, but he managed to escape his protectors and experience the "real world." He became highly developed spiritually *and* was able to adjust to "real" life. As a result, he was able to accomplish great deeds. In his book *The Gospel of St. Luke* Rudolf Steiner describes the young Jesus as having what I call an exclusively right brain mentality. He suggests that the young Jesus would be judged today as being mentally slow or somewhat retarded. Steiner does not state that Jesus was, or wasn't, intentionally raised that way. Rather, he attributes Jesus' mental state to the fact that this was Jesus' first earthly incarnation. At that time Jesus and the Christ Spirit were two distinct beings. Everything on Earth was new to him. This enabled him to have a great deal of innocence and purity. At the point in time at which Jesus had a confrontation with the money changers in the Temple he suddenly showed great maturity. This change, as expressed in the lecture series, is one of the most interesting of Steiner's revelations.

In German, "Sieg" means initiate. Sieglinde, Siegmund, and Siegfried all represent leading initiates, or composites of the leading initiates of an era. One definition of an initiate is a person who is ahead of their time. Initiates may have abilities that seem superhuman, but as everyone else matures spiritually through evolution they will reach the same stages with the same abilities. One person, even a great initiate, could not achieve all that any of Wagner's "Sieg's" does in one lifetime. Evolution is a gradual process. Parsifal, in Wagner's operas, is definitely the successor to Siegmund and Siegfried, if not, allegorically speaking, the reincarnation of Siegfried himself. Parsifal was a great initiate, and as such it would not be too surprising to learn that Wagner intended Parsifal be portrayed as having had the upbringing of an old-time initiate, although technically it would not be compatible with medieval times. Like Buddha, Parsifal was raised in a secure environment but left it of his own accord to experience the outside world.

> *Sidebar: Children, and adults, need a lot of love but should also be allowed to fight their own battles in order to become strong and grow. Parsifal and Buddha were protected from the outside world as children but since they were exceptional people they had the courage and determination to face the realities of the "world" and to rise above it. As we become stronger we will be able to do the same, but for now, we have to help others as much as we can and then let them do what they have to do on their own.*

As seen in *The Ring*, in the beginning Loge/Lucifer was very influential and powerful. But as the operas, and time, progress Alberich/Ahriman's influence becomes stronger. As Rudolf Steiner has said many times, Lucifer and Ahriman will work together when it serves their purpose. In *Parsifal*, Wagner's libretto illustrates

Ahriman using sexual instincts, basically Luciferic qualities, to achieve the goal of seducing knights so as to have them under his control. Ahriman manipulates knights through the black magician Klingsor, who uses unredeemed Luciferic powers through the sorceress Kundry. If this sounds convoluted, it is; and it is really just an example of how evil spirits work today. They have their chain of command and influence. A top dog will not waste his or her time on a neophyte; such tasks will be left for the sergeants and foot soldiers. But they do have strange bedfellows at times and will use their adversaries when it will help their cause. In this case the unredeemed Lucifer gets to exploit his sexual temptations, and Ahriman gets to control the Guardians of the Grail as they fail their tests.

Years before, Klingsor had been unsuccessful in bringing his sexual drive under control. Finally, as a last ditch effort, he emasculated himself. That did not work. He still had the sex drive but no possible means of satisfying it. Unable to deal with his lust, Klingsor's goal became to possess the Grail and use it to rule the world. As a result of his emasculation and his accompanying rage, Klingsor was able to channel his energy to the mastery of black magic (GOL, 113). With Klingsor, "The desert bloomed for him." Does this mean he became an arborist who specialized in colorful plants that needed little water? Or that he made it rain? Was he having an illusion? Were his subjects having illusions; were they in an altered state of consciousness? Or is Wagner telling us that Klingsor mastered his intellectual forces to the extent that he learned how to rule the physical world through technology? In addition Klingsor had "devilish, lovely women" to serve him in his quest to snare others into his servitude. Could this be taken as a statement that not only humanity's intellectual side was under Klingsor's control but that the Luciferic side with its sexual attraction was also being manipulated by him for his evil goals? This after all, would be part of the "fall." His situation is very similar to that of Alberich's in *The Rhinegold* who, after failing to find love with the Rhinemaidens, captures the gold and says:

> … first your men
> shall yield to my might,
> then your lovely women,
> who despise me and jeer,
> shall grant to Alberich's force
> what love could not win!
> Hahahaha!
> You have been warned!
> Beware!
> Beware of my armies of night!
> Beware the day when the Niblung's gold
> shall vanquish the world! (47)

It was through Kundry that Klingsor's lust was raised (GOL, 127). In *Parsifal* Wagner refers to her as the reincarnated Herodias. Herodias was the granddaughter of Herod the Great, wife of Herod Philip I, who was the brother of Herod Antipas. Herodias defied the law and left Philip to marry Philip's brother, Herod Antipas, who was married at the time. This was very controversial due to Jewish law but the only person to object was John the Baptist. After Herod Antipas offered Herodias' daughter, Salome (who was also his niece and stepdaughter) anything she wanted in exchange for an exotic dance, Herodias got her revenge on John by persuading her daughter Salome to ask for the head of John the Baptist on a platter. Since then Herodias/Kundry has had a tough time of it and in *Parsifal* she is still paying the price, unable to break free from Klingsor's spell.

According to Wagner's story, angels gave to Titurel, the former leader of the Knights of the Grail and the father of Amfortas', both the chalice Christ used at the Last Supper and the spear with which Longinus pierced the body of Christ. It was Titurel's task to guard them on the physical plane (GOL 112), and so he built a sanctuary which no sinners could find. This brings up an interesting point. If no sinners could find it could it have been physical objects he was guarding? If it was in the spiritual world then why did a physically incarnated person have the task of guarding it? My answer to this is that the real essence of the cup and spear had become spiritualized and that as humanity's consciousness increased, the spiritual and physical worlds became more united. In other words, the Grail is a high state of consciousness and it had to be guarded on Earth from such attacks as might come from black magic practitioners like Klingsor and/or from people who use drugs or other mind-altering techniques to enter the spiritual world from a lower state of consciousness. At the time just before Parsifal, Titurel was the earthly guardian.

As a result of the fall, what was once unity in the spiritual world has become differentiated. What we believe to be physical matter is just energy that has condensed into individualized pieces (to use terms from our earthy, intellectual vocabulary), so much so that we normally consider it distinct from spirit. But even within the physical realm matter is greatly differentiated. Take water: it can be mist, the fluid that makes up our lakes and oceans, or it can be frozen in the forms of snow or ice. The cup and the spear would belong in the physical realm for sure. However, the cup or Grail is more than a physical object. On one allegorical level it could be the chalice or container in which Joseph of Arimathea gathered the blood of Christ. The blood of Christ had very special spiritual qualities which were made available to humanity, enabling us to reach higher levels of consciousness. It is these qualities which matter, not the original physical object which was used to hold them. The Grail today is the spiritual qualities found in the blood of Christ. A clue which can leave little doubt that in *Parsifal* the Grail was in the spiritual realm is that Gurnemanz says, "Here time is one with space" (119).

In the higher allegorical sense of the Bible, Joseph of Arimathea himself was the Grail. He was of such high consciousness that he was the first to hold both the body and blood of the crucified Christ. He held the blood spiritually in his soul as well as physically in the cup. As evolution progresses others will reach that stage and become co-guardians of the Grail. The true Grail is not the physical cup. It is a higher level of consciousness. It could even be said to be our higher selves, which contain the blood of Christ.

The spear is supposed to be the Spear of Longinus, the spear that pierced the side of Christ when he hung dead on the cross. Longinus could have thrown the spear out of hatred, or he could have thrown it to keep the centurions from breaking the legs of Christ – which they would have done in order to make sure he died before sunset, to satisfy Jewish custom. If they had broken Christ's legs, they also would have broken the Old Testament prophecy that said not a bone of the messiah's body would be broken. Did Longinus throw the spear for good or for evil? A tradition came out of this, that whoever had the spear after that had control of the world, for good or evil, depending on how that person wielded their power.

According to author Trevor Ravenscroft in his book The Spear of Destiny, history has proven this tradition true, and the spear of Longinus is now in a museum in Austria. United States troops found it in a cave containing artworks stolen by the Germans just before Hitler committed suicide. Ravenscroft states that as times changed and due largely to the complexities of technology, no one person can have the power that exceptional (good or bad) individuals in the past had, and that the spear lost its power with the fall of Hitler.[25]

---

[25] As far as the cup is concerned, its precise location is not known, as far as I know. However, there is a strong possibility that it wound up in the hands of the Knights Templar. There is a very plausible theory that it was smuggled out of France, hidden in

Sidebar: According to esoteric teachings everything is spirit. What we perceive as matter is really spirit, but by perceiving it through our physical senses we have the illusion that it is physical matter and that it is separated from the spiritual world. In Eastern philosophy this is called Maya. It really does exist, but not in the form which we perceive.

Roslyn, Scotland, and – when it was considered no longer safe there – taken across the ocean and buried at Oak Harbor, Nova Scotia. An excellent book that tells about this, without being specific about the grail, is *The Lost Treasure of the Knights Templar: Solving the Oak Island Mystery* by Steven Sora. The Oak Island treasure was buried so cleverly that although its site was discovered over one hundred years ago, the treasure has never been recovered. To protect their secret the possessors of the treasure dug horizontal side shafts off the main, vertical mine shaft so as to let water flood the entire mine and foil all attempts to extricate the treasure buy unauthorized personal. However, someone had to have the key to finding it. Had they wanted to prevent the treasure from falling into the wrong hands and were not concerned with retrieving it themselves they could have dumped it in the middle of the Atlantic Ocean. They, whoever they are, wanted to be able to retrieve it when necessary or appropriate. In view of what has been discovered their hydraulic engineering feat clearly demonstrates that it would have been an easy matter to dig a side shaft towards the center of the island on an upward incline which would end above the high tide line and which would be very easy to retrieve by a person with the map digging straight down at the right place.

If Joseph of Arimathea's cup which was used at the Last Supper and later used to capture the blood of Christ is part of the treasure, the person who finds it could proclaim himself or herself to be the Guardian of the Grail and, who knows, they might even proclaim themselves to be the second coming of Christ. This is just speculation on my part but it will be interesting to see what happens if the treasure is recovered.

Titurel, according to Wagner's story, would have been the incarnated person with the highest level of consciousness at that time, so it was up to him to protect this special gift. But he grew old and sick (GOL, 113) and turned the responsibility of guarding the Grail to his son, Amfortas. But Amfortas was not strong enough to protect the spear. Kundry seduced him, and while that was happening Klingsor took the spear and used it to wound Amfortas in his side while trying to escape. The wound never healed (GOL, 111-112).

In Wagner's story Amfortas had the spear but lost it to Klingsor when the knight got caught in Kundry's seduction, and now Klingsor is determined to capture the Grail so that he can rule the world.

In the opera *Siegfried*, Siegfried fails to rise up to higher levels of consciousness because his strong will and Luciferic lust for Brünnhilde prevent her from sharing her wisdom with him. This failure enables the Ahrimanic forces under Hagen, to use Siegfried's spiritual forces for their own purposes: to attempt to acquire *the ring*, which would enable them to satisfy their desire for gold (money) and give them the power to rule the world. In *Parsifal* the Ahrimanic forces are using the Luciferic powers to achieve their goal, that of

Sidebar: Anne Catherine Emmerich states in her memoirs The Dolorous Passion of Our Lord Jesus Christ, that whatever his intentions Longinus later gave up being a centurion and became a very loyal follower of Christ

gaining possession of the Grail. By making the physical sex urge so strong that the knights are unable to pursue the goal of higher consciousness, Klingsor keeps them incapacitated while he attempts to steal the Grail.

The Grail can be used for good or evil. Klingsor/ Ahriman is not pure enough to get it on his own but he can capture it through others who are pure enough but too ignorant to know they are being manipulated. In this case the guardians of the Grail are not pure enough. Parsifal, the pure fool, is – but so far he is too ignorant to do the job. He is the last hurdle Klingsor has to overcome to gain the Grail. Klingsor recognizes Parsifal's potential, and sets forth to spoil it. Once Parsifal is under his control there will be no stopping Klingsor from attaining the Grail.

Wagner is not saying sex is wrong, but he is saying lust is wrong. He made this clear in *The Valkyrie* when Wotan and Fricka were having their discussion on the laws of marriage.

Unholy
call I the vows
that bind unloving hearts. (98)

Love is what counts, not a title or classification. In *Parsifal*, Klingsor emasculates himself. This was not the way to purity or higher consciousness, but Klingsor could not conceive of the sex act as a means of expressing a higher form of love.

Sidebar: The Spear of Destiny by Trevor Ravenscroft is another of the controversial sources I draw upon. The source of the controversy, or part of it, is that Ravenscroft made a lot of claims which the reader is led to believe were drawn from his clairvoyance. There are no secrets in the spiritual world, at least for those who have the ability or "eyes" to see into that world. Since several other conscious clairvoyants are reported to have tried to duplicate his findings without success it is believed he either had an overactive imagination or he outright lied. Nevertheless, I found parts of the book very informative.

King Amfortas is too incapacitated from his spear-wound to lead the knights. Gurnemanz is in charge. He realizes balms, balsams, and potions are not going to cure the King; it requires a special man (GOL, 107). Amfortas calls this unknown special man the one "made wise through pity" (GOL, 108) and "the blameless fool" (GOL, 109). In other words, a physical cure is not going to be found: it will take a person who has attained purity and higher consciousness to stand up to the forces of evil.

When Parsifal first encounters Gurnemanz and the other knights he is tested to see if he is the special person who is to become King of the Grail. He fails the test. Nevertheless, Klingsor knows Parsifal has the potential (GOL, 126) and wants him out of the way. Klingsor calls on Kundry. Wagner now falls back on his own life experiences to describe the following:

Parsifal comes to Klingsor's castle. He storms it, wounding all the troops that try to block his entrance and driving them off. Inside is a magic garden from which, on all sides, flower maidens rush in (GOL, 129). They are mad at Parsifal for injuring their lovers. He explains he had to fight them off because they tried to keep him from them (GOL, 131). This may sound like a cornball flirtatious remark but allegorically it indicates Parsifal was searching for higher consciousness (love). After convincing the flower maidens that he is not going to hurt them they ask who will play with them now. Of course, Parsifal says he will. The word "play" can be considered a clue that they are shallow and will not help him grow in his consciousness. He has a different idea of play. This scene is similar to what the Rhinemaidens wanted to do with Siegfried in *Twilight of the Gods* (309, 311). It is also similar to Homer's description of what happened in *The Odyssey* when Odysseus encountered Circe. He could have lived in peaceful bliss with a goddess who loved him and satisfied his needs, but there would be no future – just more of the same peaceful bliss, day in and day out, no growth, no satisfaction. In *Twilight of the Gods* the Rhinemaidens try to seduce Siegfried. He is tempted (311), but he is married and takes their description of *the ring*'s curse as a threat (309, 311). In *Parsifal*, Parsifal has passed many tests to prove he is immune from fear and when the flower maidens try to intimidate him he rejects them. The Rhinemaidens, Circe, and the flower maidens are all Luciferic tempters. They could give everything a person could want except for growth into higher consciousness. To give in to them would mean sacrificing the future for an ongoing present nirvana, but with a very questionable happiness. Luciferic temptations are used in many spiritually allegorical stories. In today's world this can be compared to people who are obsessed with safety and security rather than inner growth.

In *Twilight of the Gods* Siegfried turns down the Rhinemaidens because he thinks they threaten rather than woo him. In *The Odyssey*, Odysseus rejects Circe because he misses his wife (higher consciousness, soul). In *Parsifal*, Parsifal rejects the flower maidens because he realizes that since each one selfishly wants him at the expense of the others their love is shallow. None of these heroes is going to accept second best.

The regular knights were an easy target for the flower maidens, but Parsifal is not a regular knight. He has been on a quest for higher consciousness and has experienced life, with its many varied forms of testing. The flower maidens are no challenge for him. But Klingsor is prepared. He now brings in his "ace in the hole," Kundry. She is in a class way above the immature flower maidens and will do what they could not. As Parsifal is about to flee from the garden she appears. She tells the flower maidens "with their fast-withering flowers" that "he was not sent for [their] sport" (GOL, 136). They get the message, take a couple of cheap shots at Parsifal, and depart.

Kundry starts with a much more sophisticated approach than that of the flower maidens. Although she is very beautiful now, Kundry knows that beauty of any magnitude will not overpower Parsifal's disdain for casual sex. She knows Parsifal's weakness and immediately, but very subtly, goes for it. Parsifal is too strong to yield to temptations to his lower nature, so she will try to manipulate him through his higher consciousness.

Parsifal is frightened by Kundry (in a way similar to Siegfried's initial fear of Brünnhilde) and wants to know if she is a flower? To relate this to the world today, he may be strong but he is in an altered state of consciousness. In spite of his moral strength he is vulnerable. She says that she is not a flower maiden and proceeds to tenderly tell him about what he has been searching for: she tells him of his father's death and how his mother tried to protect him from "men in deadly conflict." She says that she was with his father when he died (GOL, 137). She knows his weakness. She tells Parsifal that she saw his mother caring tenderly for him, and that she saw how grieved his mother was by the death of his father. She tells him that his mother strove to protect him from his father's fate and thus allowed no talk of fighting to reach him. Kundry tells Parsifal how happy his mother was every time he returned from his roaming. She tells him how his mother, beginning the day that Parsifal did not return, waited for a long time. She tells him that eventually his mother's grief got the best of her and she died of a broken heart. This gets to core of Parsifal's quest. He now realizes his responsibility and takes blame for his mother's death. Feelings of guilt and heartache consume him.

All this can be taken on several allegorical levels. The death of his mother could be a reference to historical personalities on which the Parsifal story is based. It could refer to the fictitious earthly mother of the main character. Or since Mother, in esoteric literature, refers to the soul (i.e. the inner, personal, spiritual qualities within each person), it could refer to the death of part of him, his higher self, as he succumbs to the world of intellectual parts-and-pieces which I call "the fall."

Most people faced with temptations such as those Parsifal experiences, would give in to a lower state of consciousness and allow their feelings to reign. Lower consciousness seems easily accessible when under duress, but as I have tried to say throughout this book, lower consciousness is the domain in which freedom is lost and a person becomes a slave to their emotions. Kundry, having done all that she can to manipulate Parsifal into such a state now makes her big move.

She tells him that because he has experienced such grief he can now raise himself up to the joy that love can reveal. She is appealing to his higher consciousness, and there is a lot to be said for her argument. Even Rudolf Steiner's teachings say a person's ability to rise up into the spiritual world is dependent upon the amount of pain and suffering they have experienced. Here is where Kundry's wisdom and seductive power really go to work.

Kundry tells Parsifal, "Acknowledge your fault, and then it's ended; by knowledge your folly soon is mended." There is a lot to this. In Chapters 4 and 7, I wrote about the Guardian of the Threshold and how it is portrayed in Wagner's opera *Siegfried*. By facing up to our dark side we can move on to our higher side. I have previously discussed the value of dealing with our problems on an intellectual level rather than an emotional level. The "acknowledgement" that Kundry encourages could be an example of both these higher acts of consciousness.

Parsifal is already highly emotionally aroused from Kundry's revelations. Kundry brilliantly continues working on Parsifal's weakness, telling him that he can now experience the "rapture" (GOL, 139) that his father felt for Parsifal's mother and which gave him life. "(Love) sends you now a mother's blessing, greets a son with love's first kiss!" She kisses Parsifal on the lips. This is an example of the forces of evil using the truth to win a person's emotions and confidence. But then, having won confidence and trust, they attempt to steer their victim astray.

Yes, Parsifal can now achieve a higher state of spiritual consciousness, but Kundry wants to seduce Parsifal and enslave him to a lower state of consciousness, where he will be subjected to the commands of Klingsor. She has played Parsifal perfectly. How could he resist? Who in Parsifal's condition wouldn't be ready to experience the love Kundry proposes? I can only imagine what Wagner must have gone through to achieve the spiritual wisdom he embeds in this scene. But rather than yield to his lower emotions, Parsifal rises to higher consciousness. He puts his hand to his heart and experiences the pain Amfortas has in his heart from the spear (GOL, 139). He feels the pain of Christ and asks, "Redeemer! Savior! Lord of grace! Can I my sinful crime efface?" (GOL, 140). Kundry is astonished by this. But she doesn't give up. She pushes on. Standing above Parsifal she tells him to look up and find redemption. He pushes her away (GOL, 141).

Kundry tries a new approach. She begs him to save her. She admits she saw Him (Christ) and mocked him. She says she continually sought forgiveness but failed to find it. She says that if she could be united with him for just one hour she would be redeemed (GOL, 142). She has changed her tactic from playing on his emotions over his mother, to making a personal plea for salvation. Parsifal says they would be condemned together. He says he was sent for her salvation but she must repent. But she keeps at him. The full embrace of her loving will bring him to the godhead (GOL, 143). He can redeem the world by accepting her love, even though she will remain condemned. This continues. He wants to know where Amfortas is. She tells Parsifal she will take him to Amfortas after one hour with Parsifal. He pushes her away as she attempts to embrace him again.

She realizes she is losing the battle. She will summon the spear. She curses Parsifal to have to wander forever as she has had to do.

Suddenly Klingsor appears. He throws the spear at Parsifal saying "The holy fool will fall by his master's spear!" (GOL, 144). But Parsifal catches the spear in mid-air. In *Siegfried*, Siegfried broke Wotan's spear showing he was stronger than the old gods. In *Parsifal*, Parsifal doesn't break Klingsor's spear. He captures it and has its power to use as he sees fit. Klingsor's enchantment is ended. His castle falls. The garden becomes a desert again. Parsifal tells Kundry she knows where to find him if she wants him, and the scene changes.

Gurnemanz is old; Kundry is near death (GOL, 145). She is dressed as a penitent and seeks to serve. Gurnemanz tells her that messengers, like she used to be, are no longer needed, the knights have to find herbs and roots for themselves now. Parsifal appears in black armor with his visor down. Gurnemanz tells him it is Good Friday and to lay down his weapons. He does, and lifts his visor at which time he is recognized. When asked how he found his way there Parsifal replies:

Through error and through suffering's pathways came I ...
I wandered in error,
by a fearful curse led astray;
numberless dangers,
battles, and duels
forced me to leave the pathway,
even when I thought it was found.
Then I was seized with dread of failure,
to keep the Spear unprofaned;
so to defend it, and to guard it,
I suffered many a wound on the way,

the Spear itself
could not be wielded in battle;
unprofaned
at my side then I bore it;
and home I now restore it:
you see it shining pure and clear -
the Grail's most holy Spear. (GOL, 148)

Parsifal has won the spear, but his ordeal is not over. His task is now to guard and protect the spear. It cannot be used in anger against his enemies. After many years of successfully doing this he happens to come across Gurnemanz and Kundry again. Kundry is old and repentant. Gurnemanz accepts Parsifal now as the new king. The scene gradually changes and the forest is replaced with a rock wall (GOL, 153). The wall opens and behind it is the Grail Hall. The rock's opening suggests that they have transcended the laws of physics and entered the spiritual world. Parsifal takes the spear, touches Amfortas' wound with it, and Amfortas is cured. Parsifal then goes to the altar takes the chalice, which grows brighter as a dove descends and hovers over his head (GOL, 156), signifying that he has reached a higher, divine, state of consciousness, one that we will eventually reach. The final curtain descends.

The question is often asked, "What is the Holy Grail?" Answers are usually vague at best. My take is as follows:

Anne Catherine Emmerich, in the book The Life of Christ gives a very interesting account of Christ's approach to Earth for his physical incarnation. She tells of the ancient Jews first being conscious of a "holy thing" through the burning bush (the realm of fire). Later it was through the Ark of the Covenant, then the Temple. Steiner would refer to this "holy thing" as Christ. An important point is that it was not perceived in a once-and-for-all-time manifestation; it evolved. Then, according to Christian teachings, Mary became the vehicle when she was pregnant, and, next it was through Jesus when he was born. However, at this time, according to Steiner, Christ had not incarnated into the body of Jesus. The actual incarnation would take place at the Baptism in the Jordan. From that point on Jesus was the home or dwelling of Christ. Christ referred to his body as his Temple. At the Last Supper he let it be known that the bread (physical realm) and wine (fluid realm) were also his body and blood. The chalice that held his blood that night (from which he and his disciples drank) is often referred to as the Grail. At his death Christ left the body of Jesus and the entire earth became his body. Emmerich says that Joseph of Arimathea gathered his spilt blood and took his body down from the cross, making him the first one to take the body and blood of Christ after his death. Steiner made it very clear that Christ had incarnated once and would never again incarnate on the physical plane. The Second Coming would be in higher, etheric realms. Christ can no longer work on an individual level. However, as we progress we enter spiritual realms in our consciousness and become a bridge between the two worlds. Christ can work with us on our higher levels, and He can then be expressed through us on the lower level where He cannot work directly.

Lucifer is known as the light bearer. He does not have a light of his own but the light of Christ does shine through him. That is, through the higher side of Lucifer. But Lucifer fell and Christ cannot shine through him in a fallen state. Lucifer is in us, we cannot escape that. It is up to us to redeem him by purifying our lower nature. When we do that we change our relationship with him to that of the higher Lucifer, the true light bearer.

As we do that we unite with that higher side we unite with his qualities and we, through Lucifer, become light bearers. Our temples, our bodies, now become a home for Christ to shine through. At this stage we will be the guardians of the Grail.

THE CONTINUING BATTLE

The objectives of those opposed to the development of higher consciousness (evolution) have not changed throughout history. In this epilogue I will highlight some of the more powerful tools that have been used to manipulate and control people, at the expense of human freedom.

Humans "fell" from the spiritual world because we could not keep up with more advanced spirits. They were advancing too fast for us, creating a heat that would have destroyed us. By entering the world of parts-and-pieces, where things happen more slowly, humanity eventually learned to examine details; something the higher spirits could not do. From that experience we became creative, but our creativity was limited to the physical world. Finding "god" again would have to wait. For a long time, we would have to be satisfied with clergymen and gurus, and all sorts of other self-appointed experts who would tell their followers that heaven (the best we can hope for) is a return to the state which existed before the fall. Or they might say that to get there one just has to be good; or just believe. Or they might teach that, in effect, the spiritual world is just a less condensed extension of the physical world. Most of these leaders did not, and do not, know the difference between the unconscious state which existed

before the fall and the fully conscious state which evolution is leading us toward.

In the third cultural epoch we acquired the physical
senses and became enslaved to our feelings. Humanity
of that era was in no way free. Siegmund and Sieglinde
allegorically represent early people who try to overcome
that state. They fail, but their efforts set the stage for
the next generation. Siegfried allegorically represents
the leading thinkers of that next generation, the fourth
cultural epoch. This was an epoch over which the archangel Michael presided[26]. His task was to implement
intelligence, since the physical senses were fully opera-
tional. Historically, this epoch aligns with the Greek
philosophers and the rise of analytical thinking. Until
that time, most philosophers used thinking only to
try to understand the spiritual world, an intent that
becomes obvious when reading their works. Aristotle
was the first philosopher to use thinking to explain
the physical world. Raphael's painting "The School of
Athens" illustrates this very clearly: Aristotle's teacher,
Plato, is pointing up to the heavens but Aristotle's hand
is palm down indicating the earth must be considered.
Understanding the physical world was a big and necessary step for humanity, but in many ways it turned out
to be too much of a good thing. Our connection to the
spiritual world was lost or at least distorted. Michael's
rule ended with Aristotle. The next archangel had a
different task. There would be no further incentive or

---

[26] Rudolf Steiner (1861-1925) taught that the 2,160-year cycle
is further divided into cycles of a little over 300 years. These are
periods led by some of the leading archangels and archais.

help to explore the spiritual world through thinking until Michael's next term, beginning in 1879. With few exceptions (mostly heretics who became martyrs, and the Scholastics Albertus Magnus and his student St. Thomas Aquinas) thinking remained in the realm of the physical world.

Throughout the next two millennia religious and secular leaders strove to suppress thinking. If thinking could be suppressed or eliminated people would be slaves to emotions and, in that condition, more easily controlled, primarily through the use of force and fear. Some religions were adamant about not trying to cross over into God's domain: people showing signs of clairvoyance were likely be executed for being heretics.

Side bar: In his lecture series "Building Blocks of the Mystery of Golgotha," Rudolf Steiner relates how the early church manipulated people. Initiates in the various mystery centers had rituals to help them on their spiritual paths. Eventually the Church and Roman leaders learned about these rituals, then co-opted and perverted them, so as to manipulate people into becoming dependent on the Roman Empire through its subsidiary, the Church. These rituals have come down to us as the present day sacraments. The church increased its influence through design, dogma, and restrictions on education. In spite of their corruption and manipulation the Church did keep the idea of the spiritual world alive at a time when people did not have the mental capacity to understand the spiritual world. In this respect the Church performed a very useful task.

The Age of Enlightenment arrived with the 19th century. Leaders believed that thinking on the physical level was the highest form of consciousness. It was believed thinking originated in and was a product of the brain. God became nothing more than a childish belief. In mid-century, Wagner hinted at the need for consciousness of the spiritual world, but it was not until Rudolf Steiner wrote the book *The Philosophy of Freedom* (ca. 1898) that a philosopher explained it could indeed be done. In his subsequent book *Knowledge of Higher Worlds and Its Attainment* he explained how a person could do it. Michael's next term began in 1879. It took a while for results of this to begin surfacing. Rudolf Steiner's works were early examples.

In *The Philosophy of Freedom* Steiner explains that thinking is, indeed, a spiritual activity, not a physical one, and that the world of ideas can be observed just as clearly as physical objects are observed. This idea broke the existing barrier between the physical world and the spiritual world, at least for those who had the ability to fathom it. Steiner explains that because of our intimacy with thinking and concepts we can actually know the world of spirit even better than we can know the physical world. Unfortunately, *The Philosophy of Freedom* could not be written until the very end of the 19th century, and even then few people would read it. Even fewer would have the flexibility of thinking necessary to comprehend it. But that is getting ahead of the story.

One of the most important mainstream philosophers of Wagner and Steiner's time was Georg Wilhelm

Frederic Hegel (1770-1831). Hegel reasoned that emotions were limited to an individual. Someone might come along and scare you and me, but your fear is yours and only yours, mine is mine and only mine. Hegel taught that emotions are an individual phenomenon but that thinking is universal. If you think of an apple and I think of an apple we are thinking of the same concept or idea. You may have a degree in botany and understand apples better than I, but this is only a matter of degree; we are both thinking about the same concept. Therefore, he said, thoughts and concepts are universal. Being universal they have to be a higher form of consciousness than feelings, which are limited to individuals. So far so good. Hegel could only take his brilliant conclusion so far. The end result was that he reasoned that the ultimate form of thought was not in the spiritual realm but in the realm of government. The government was a meeting of minds and so, Hegel concluded, it represented the highest form of consciousness available to man. Therefore, he reasoned, humans were meant to be subjects of the state. In his book *Riddles of Philosophy* Rudolf Steiner explains this very succinctly.

Hegel's philosophy led a movement which believed that people should be subjects of the state, and that if they resisted, intentionally or not, they should be coerced or forced to toe the line.[27] Shortly after Hegel's time Abraham Lincoln said government should be by

---

[27]In *The Philosophy of Freedom* Steiner many times refutes the arguments of Eduard von Hartmann. Hartmann was the leading advocate of Hegelian philosophy at that time. Hegel's philosophy

the people, of the people and for the people. But he was soon assassinated.

After that Lincoln's idea of government was given a great deal of lip service in the United States, but the followers of Hegel's philosophy were working for a long term takeover of world governments, beginning with the United States. Antony C. Sutton documents in detail how this happened in his eye-opening book *America's Secret Establishment*. The way people were to be controlled was by presenting people two conflicting arguments in a way that brings about managed change, just as Hegel advocated. This method is called dialectic; the two sides of the dialectic are called thesis and antithesis. The clash of these sides brings about the synthesis (Sutton 34). By presenting a subjectively predetermined thesis and antithesis the synthesis can also be predetermined. Hegel's proponents did not care which side predominated, since either one would serve their goal of reaching a pre-selected synthesis. It was a brilliant way to manipulate the masses.

To Hegel's philosophy was added the experimental psychology of Wilhelm Maximilian Wundt (1832-1920). This is especially significant because of its extreme influence on the American education system (Sutton 90-91). Wundt believed that people were not free by nature. He theorized that actions and thoughts were the result of past experiences, and that people were pawns who required guidance.

---

would have a major impact on the future, and there should be no doubt Steiner was trying to warn the world about its dangers.

Sidebar: I have to wonder if Wagner was not referring to Hegel when he named Hagen, in Twilight of the Gods. Hagen was a bad guy, however, while Hegel was a good guy, just limited in his thinking, despite being a leading thinker of his time. That a lot of harm came from his ideas does not make him an evil person. Nevertheless, Wagner may not have been so charitable in his opinion of Hegel. It should be pointed out that Rudolf Steiner had great admiration for Hegel. Steiner recognized that he took human thinking to the next level, and although Hegel could not go beyond that (and others would use his findings for decadent purposes), Hegel did perform a great service for humanity with his philosophical determination that thinking was a higher form of consciousness than feeling.

Sutton's book focuses a great deal on the Order of Skull and Bones at Yale College, which later became Yale University. He explains how three members of this organization studied in Germany, and then returned to the United States with Hegelian beliefs firmly entrenched. They set about systematically forming or infiltrating organizations that control nearly every important aspect of American culture – from history books, to religion, to medicine, to education, to the press, and government – and through hundreds of doctoral graduates, Hegelian philosophy became ingrained in American institutions. Their success was nothing less than phenomenal. Installed in positions of power, members of the Order maintained control in keeping with their view of people as servants of the state, which they and their cronies were positioned to run. This is not to say that all members of the Order of Skull and Bones were devils incarnate. Many were very sincere, but sincerity does not always translate into noble actions. One of the appealing aspects of Hegelian philosophy was that its adherents would have the opportunity to be leaders and wield a great deal of influence and power. It could be a real ego trip.

The Order of Skull and Bones today has outlived its usefulness. Their secrets are out, and once secrets are discovered secret organizations become impotent; however, it is standard procedure to start up a new secret organization when an old one is fading. Skull and Bones is no longer a threat but the new organization of plutocracy, whatever it is called, will have a similar agenda.

So far, I have touched on the tools of fear and indoctrination. Both have been used to manipulate the masses, sometimes through institutions and leaders who have the appearance of social respectability. I now turn to topics related to explicit mind control programs that were kept highly secret until fairly recently.

The theory of mind control may go back to the late 1770s, when Franz Anton Mesmer developed therapeutic techniques that would become the basis for hypnosis. At the core of hypnosis are tools and skills for focusing a person's attention on feelings or other right brain matters, which block the intellect. Without intellect present, individuality becomes suppressed. A person becomes very suggestible. As long as suggestions are given in a way that does not appear to go against a person's basic beliefs they can be very powerful, and a smart operator can get around some people's basic beliefs. The problem today is not so much the neighborhood hypnotist who tries to help a person control their weight or stop smoking, although they are still conditioning a person to relinquish their willpower at a time when humanity needs to be developing a stronger will. The problem is when variations of this technique are used more subtly.

The manipulation of mob psychology is an example of this. People love being at a rock concert and just becoming part of the crowd, or attending a sporting event where their emotions go wild with the crowd. At such times people are more open to subconscious influences, and advertisers are well aware of this. Their techniques, and those of other manipulators, are so sophisticated that it takes a real individual to resist them all. In 1974, William Bryan Key published *Subliminal Persuasion*, in which he disclosed a great deal of information on the subject of mass manipulation. It came as a shock to many to discover that in movie theaters a single film frame, which takes one fifth of a second and is too fast for the conscious mind to grasp, flashed the words "drink soda" and "eat popcorn" with astounding results. These results were very easy to tabulate and it was determined the sales of soda and popcorn went up substantially after the subconscious manipulation. It did not make any particular person run to the snack counter, but those who had developed a liking for soda and popcorn were easy prey. What could not be assimilated by the conscious mind was readily assimilated by the unconscious mind. The higher level of consciousness one has developed the less likely one is to be susceptible.

In the 1950s the CIA and the U.S. military started formally experimenting with mind control. What the CIA wanted was to develop people who could be given secret information that could not be recalled in consciousness. If caught by enemy agents, these specially-programmed agents could not be forced to disclose information, even under torture. The data would only be made accessible to a person who had the secret word or formula that would trigger their memory and program them to release the information. Information about the United States' mind control programs that ran from 1950-1984 has now been declassified.

From 1953-1963, the CIA's mind control program was called MKULTRA. It used drugs, hypnosis, and electronic means to manipulate people who had been selected as good candidates for mind control. People working in this field determined that the best subject was a person with a dissociative identity disorder (formerly known as split personality disorder). This condition describes people who can temporarily or permanently block their consciousness in a way that suppresses memory. Trauma survivors and childhood sexual abuse survivors often have developed mental skills that block out experiences that are too harsh to face. People who already have the ability to block out certain aspects of their lives can be relatively easily programmed and are easy prey for people interested in mind control. Excellent books on this subject are *The CIA's Control of Candy Jones* by Donald Bain and *Trance Formation* by Mark Phillips and Cathy O'Brien.

Candy Jones developed a split personality as a child in order to deal with her mother's repressive treatment. Cathy O'Brien was a victim of childhood sexual abuse and had learned to block out incidents which were too traumatic to bring to consciousness. Both women became unwitting participants in CIA or government-sponsored mind control programs. These were two exceptional people who, with the help of their spouses, were able to rise above the abuse and manipulations that were imposed upon them and reclaim their individuality. As Cathy O'Brien's husband Mark Phillips points out, the solution is to face up to the past by thinking it out without getting emotionally involved. Bringing the intellect to the fore reduces the traumatic impact of emotional responses associated with a harsh reality, and that allows the individual to remain present and in control of their actions. Both these women were able to break free of official mind control programs by using their intellect. Their stories illustrate higher consciousness being applied with great effect in the battle for individual freedom.

The purpose of the above discussion is to emphasize that the objectives of those opposed to the development of higher consciousness have not changed throughout history. The difference is in the sophistication of their tactics and the technologies available.

The predatory wild animal looks for the weakest prey, the neighborhood bully looks for weak prey; manipulators look for weak prey. The way to defeat them is to not be weak. The tools are available. In many of his books Rudolf Steiner has given mental exercises to increase our consciousness. He even dedicated one book, *Knowledge of Higher Worlds and Its Attainment,* to that purpose. Steiner's methods are safe, which not all methods are, and, for the most part simple, although they do require discipline and patience.

Earlier in this book I explained how the archangel Michael was the leading spirit during years when the Greek philosophers made such amazing strides in the realm of thinking. After Michael's term was over other spirits took their turns with other agendas, and thinking was reduced from the spiritual realm to the mundane world. The closest people could come to the spiritual world was to try not to "sin" and if they really wanted to pursue the spiritual world to go into isolation in a monastery or a cave to reach a mystical, Luciferic, dreamlike experience of the spiritual world. In 1879 Michael, no longer an archangel but an archai, became the ruling spirit again. His task still has to do with thinking and consciousness but this time it is to enable us to attain cosmic consciousness, as opposed to the old mystical experiences or being limited to thinking only about physical phenomenon. Our spiritual guides are there for us. Are we ready?

BIBLIOGRAPHY

Bain, Donald. *The CIA's Control of Candy Jones.* Barricade Books, 2003.

Diamond, Jared. *Guns, Germs and Steel.* New York: W.W. Norton, 1999.

Emmerich, Anne Catherine. *The Dolorous Passion of Our Lord Jesus Christ,* translated by Clemens Maria Brentano. New York: Barnes & Noble, 2005. (Originally published in 1833.)

Hanson, Victor David. *Carnage and Culture.* Free Press, 2002.

Homer, and Stanley Lombardo. *The Odyssey.* Indianapolis: Hackett Publishing, 2000.

Key, Wilson Bryan. *Subliminal Persuasion.* Signet, 1974. ISBN 978-0451061485.

O'Brien, Cathy and Mark Phillips. *Trance Formation of America.* Reality Marketing Inc., Available for purchase online at: www.trance-formation.com.

Reeves, Nicholas. *Akhenaten: Egypt's False Prophet.* London: Thames and Hudson, 2005.

Salmon, Harry. *Initiation in the Social World.* Contact the Seattle Rudolf Steiner Books Store. www.nwrsbs.com/.

Sora, Stephen. *The Lost Treasure of the Knights Templar: Solving the Oak Island Mystery.* Rochester, VT: Destiny Books, 1999.

Steiner, Rudolf. *The Gospel of St. Luke.* London: Rudolf Steiner Press, 1964. Available free of charge online at the Rudolf Steiner Archive: http://wn.rsarchive.org/Lectures/GospLuke/GosLuk_index.html.

—*Knowledge of Higher Worlds and Its Attainment.* Spring Valley, NY: The Anthroposophic Press, 1947. Available free of charge online at: http://wn.rsarchive.org/Books/GA010/English/AP1947/GA010_index.html.

—*Mystery of Golgotha.* London: The Anthroposophical Publishing Company, 1926. Available free of charge online at: http://wn.rsarchive.org/Lectures/MysGol_index.html.

—*An Outline of Occult Science.* Spring Valley, NY: The Anthroposophic Press, 1972. Available free of charge online at: http://wn.rsarchive.org/Books/GA013/English/AP1972/GA013_index.html

—*A Philosophy of Freedom: Intuitive Thinking as a Spiritual Path,* translated by Michael Lipson. Hudson, NY: Anthroposophic Press, 1986. The previous translation of this text was published as *The Philosophy of Spiritual Activity.*

—*The Philosophy of Spiritual Activity.* Hudson, NY: Anthroposophic Press, 1986. This edition is a translation of *Die Philosophie der Freiheit.* The German volume is number four in The Collected Edition of Rudolf Steiner's works, translated by William Lindeman.

—*The Philosophy of Spiritual Activity.* Bristol: Rudolf Steiner Press, 1992. This edition is from a translation of *Die Philosophie der Freiheit* by Rita Stebbing. The German volume is number four in The Collected Edition of Rudolf Steiner's works, translated by William Lindeman.

—*Riddles of Philosophy.* Spring Valley, NY: The Anthroposophic Press, 1973. Available free of charge online at the Rudolf Steiner Archive: http://wn.rsarchive.org/Books/GA018/English/AP1973/GA018_index.html

—*The Spiritual Hierarchies: Their Reflection in the Physical World.* New York: Anthroposophic Press, 1928. Available free of charge online at the Rudolf Steiner Archive: http://wn.rsarchive.org/Lectures/SpirHier/SpiHie_index.html

—*The Temple Legend,* translated by John M. Wood from notes unrevised by the lecturer. London: Rudolf Steiner Press, 1985. The original German text is published in the Complete Edition of the works of Rudolf Steiner, *Die Tempellegende un die Goldene Legende,* No. 93 in the Bibliographical Survey.

—*Theosophy: An Introduction to the Supersensible Knowledge of the World and the Destination of Man.* Anthroposophic Press, 1971. Available online at: http://wn.rsarchive.org/Books/GA009/English/ AP1971/GA009_index.html

Sutton, Antony C. *America's Secret Establishment.* Chicago: TrineDay, 2002.

Wagner, Richard. *The Ring of the Nibelung,* translated by Andrew Porter. New York: W.W. Norton & Co., 1976.

—*Parsifal,* translated by Andrew Porter, London: Artellus Limited, 1986. Reproduced in *German Opera Libretti,* a volume in *The German Library,* New York: The Continuum Publishing Company, 1995.

CAST OF CHARACTERS

FROM THE RING CYCLE

Alberich, a Nibelung. The one who steals the gold from the Rhinemaidens and sets the opera in motion. (See: Ahriman in Steiner's Cast of Characters)

Brünnhilde, a Valkyrie. Wotan's beloved daughter

Erda, earth spirit. Mother of Brünnhilde.

Fasolt and **Fafner**, giants, spiritual creatures.

Freia, a goddess. Fricka's sister, whom Wotan pledges as payment to the Giants who build Valhalla

Fricka, a goddess. Wife of Wotan. Ruler of marriage and family.

Grane, animal. Brünnhilde's horse.

Gunther, a human. Half-brother to Alberich's son, Hagen.

Gutrune, a human. Sister to Gunther.

Hagen, a human. Son of Alberich and a woman.

Hunding, a human enslaved to Fricka. Husband to Sieglinde.

Loge, a spirit. Characterized by light and fire, guile and deceit. (See: Lucifer in Steiner's Cast of Characters)

Mime, a Niblung. Alberich's brother. He raises Siegfried.

Nibelheim, a domain. The underworld; literally, "the land of the mist."

Niblung, spiritual beings from the underworld.

Rhinemaidens, spiritual beings, eternally young.

Siegfried, son of Sieglinde and Sigmund

Sieglinde, a human. Sigmund's consort. Daughter of Wotan and a human mother.

Siegmund, a human. Son of Wotan and a human mother.

Valhalla, a domain. The castle Wotan has had built as a resting place for both the gods and his fallen earthly warriors.

Valkyrie, spiritual beings. The daughters of Wotan and the earth goddess, Erda.

Wanderer. See: Wotan.

Wotan, a god. Leader of the gods whose era is passing. Once Wotan ascends to a higher spiritual realm he becomes known as the Wanderer.

FROM PARSIFAL

Amfortas, a human. Son of Titurel. Ruler of the Kingdom of the Grail.

Gurnemanze, a human. A veteran Knight of the Grail.

Klingsor, a black magician.

Kundry, sorceress.

Parsifal, a human. The pure fool who becomes the King of the Grail.

Titurel, a human. Former ruler of the Kingdom of the Grail. Father to Amfortas.

FROM RUDOLF STEINER'S WRITINGS AND OTHER ESOTERIC LITERATURE

Able, biblical figure, human. Son of Adam and Eve.

Ahriman, a fallen archangel. Also a spirit of darkness. Also Satan.

Cain biblical figure, human. Son of Adam and Eve.

Guardian of the Threshold, a spiritual creature formed by our thoughts. It protects us from premature entry to the spiritual world.

Longinus, biblical figure, centurion who thrust his spear into the side of Christ when he hung dead on the cross.

Lucifer, biblical figure, fallen angel.

Mani, historical figure, human. Founder of the Manicheans.

Michael, biblical figure, archangel. Now archai.

"When this has come home to us; namely, that more — much more — was living in Wagner than he himself was conscious of, we must at the same time not forget that Wagner was never able to reach the last stages of wisdom. On this account the art of Richard Wagner has for the occultist quite a unique character; for while he knows that something more, something of deep mystery, is hidden behind it, he knows on the other hand that one can be in danger of looking in Wagner for something that is not there."

Rudolf Steiner
29 July 1906

Breinigsville, PA USA
04 February 2011
254847BV00001B/1/P